SHOWING OTHERS THE WAY TO HEAVEN

(A Layman's Guide to Effective Evangelism)

BY

WAYNE A. STOCKSTILL

Forward by Dr. Bruce Hitchcock

Showing Others The Way to Heaven

ISBN: 9781793182289

Table of Contents

FORWARD

In a 2014 study conducted by Baylor Religion Surveys, Baylor University, 2007, State of American Theology under the direction of Lifeway Research, 2014, the researchers found that "70% of those attending church one or more times a month never share their faith with a stranger."[1] In the same study, "51% of U.S. churchgoers say they've never heard of the term, "The Great Commission". In this survey, they also discovered that, "60% of churchgoers don't believe that sharing their faith is an essential obligation of their Christian life."

These are disturbing statistics. The Great Commission as given by Christ Jesus is found in (Matthew 28:18-20, NKJV) and states, "And Jesus came and spoke to them, saying, "All authority has been given to Me in heaven and on earth. Go therefore* and make disciples of all the nations, baptizing them in the name of the Father and of the Son and of the Holy Spirit, teaching them to observe all things that I have commanded you; and lo, I am with you always, even to the end of the age." Amen. In a related scripture, Acts 1:8 (NIV), Jesus says, "But you will receive power when the Holy Spirit comes on you; and you will be my witnesses in Jerusalem, and in all Judea and Samaria, and to the ends of the earth."

Being a witness for Jesus by sharing the gospel message is not a good suggestion it is a command. Sharing the good news of Christ birth, life, death, burial, resurrection, and ascension is essential to the growth of Christianity in the world. Without

---

[1] Outside the Walls, *This Week's Shocking Stat*, © Copyright 2018 Revival Outside the Walls, rotw.com/get-facts/70-those-attending-church-one-or-more-times-month-never-share-their-faith-stranger-0

witnesses, fundamental evangelical Christianity will cease as we know it today.

In his book "Showing Others the Way to Heaven:" A Layman's Guide to Effective Evangelism, Wayne Stockstill explains the "ins and outs" of evangelism. This book is educational, inspirational, instructional, relational. It is the most complete handbook on the who's, why's, where's, what's, when's, and how's that I have seen or read.

This book is a must read.

Dr. Bruce Hitchcock

GIVE US A WATCHWORD FOR THE HOUR,

A THRILLING WORD, A WORD OF POWER;

A BATTLE-CRY, A FLAMING BREATH,

A CALL TO CONQUEST OR TO DEATH,

A WORD TO ROUSE THE CHURCH FROM REST,

TO HEED THE MASTER'S HIGH BEHEST.

THE CALL IS GIVEN: YE HOST ARISE,

OUR WATCHWORD IS EVANGELIZE!

TO DYING MEN, A FALLEN RACE,

MAKE KNOWN THE GIFT OF GOSPEL GRACE;

THE WORLD THAT NOW IN DARKNESS LIES,

EVANGELIZE! EVANGELIZE!

--HENRY CROCKER

PREFACE

I once heard a great evangelistic sermon that was based on the training that was given to all the salespersons of a certain business (Westinghouse Corporation). The training showed that to be a successful salesperson one had to answer four questions: What is your product? What does your product do? Who says that it does? How can I get it?

We need to be clear in our understanding what it is that we are offering people. If it is not clear to our minds, how can it ever be clear to the minds of the hearers?

> Our Product: Abundant life on earth and eternity with God in heaven.
>
> What our product does: Forgiveness of sins, new creations, peace beyond human understanding.
>
> Who guarantees our product: Eternal life guaranteed by God and evidenced by the Holy Spirit.
>
> How to get our product: All ours free for the asking, mingled with faith in Jesus Christ.

Our product is a life of abundance on earth and eternal life in the heavens with God through faith in Jesus Christ. We are not offering a life free from problems, but a life with the Great Problem Solver inside us. We are not offering an amelioration (easing) of one's feelings, but an amazing transformation of life on earth and in eternity. We are not offering a salving of the conscience, but a satisfaction of the righteous judgment of God upon sinners. We are not offering a denial of guilt, but a removal of guilt.

Our product brings the forgiveness of sins, the new creation of the person, a position in Christ Jesus, peace beyond human understanding, and fellowship with God and His people. We are offering guidance for daily living, strength for temptation, communication with God, and faith to face death without fear.

Our product is guaranteed by God. It is evidenced by His Holy Spirit living inside us. He says that He will do these things, and He can never lie. Millions of fellow believers also testify to the validity of our product. Once you accept Him, you will also get the evidence: "If anyone wants to do His will, he will understand whether the teaching is from God or if I am speaking on My own" (John 7: 17).

The way to get this product is to accept it as a free gift of God's grace. It cannot be purchased, earned by good works, assimilated from religion, or claimed by family relationship. It requires repentance of sin and faith in the Lord Jesus Christ.

That is why I have written this work on evangelism—the telling forth of the Good News of salvation through faith in the Lord Jesus Christ. I am sharing these words after more than 66 years of public ministry, specializing in the field of evangelism. This volume if followed will help you fulfill the Great Commandment and the Great Commission. May God add His blessings to these words.

I want to express my deep appreciation to those who have mentored me. I also wish to express deep thanks to those who have believed in me and invited me to work alongside them in their endeavors for the Kingdom of God. Thanks to Gloria, my wife, and to my two children, Jonathan and Cynthia, for supporting me in this work—they sacrificed time with me so I could travel the world and spread the Good News of Jesus Christ. I hope and pray that my feet have been "beautiful" to those who have heard me.

My sincere desire is that this book will help you become an effective evangelist. I want to immediately acknowledge that I have made no attempt to be original. Much of these materials has been gathered from notes in college, seminary, seminars, and books by such men as Gordon Johnson, C.E. Matthews, C. S. Lovett, Roland G. Leavell, F. Carlton Booth, Ralph W. Neighbor, Jr., George Sweazey, Ian MacPherson, Charles G. Finney, D. L. Moody, Charles Haddon Spurgeon, Alexander MacClaren, John R. W. Stott, Jesse M. Bader, Dr. Charles McClain, F. D. Whitsell, E.Y. Mullins, F. Alan Streett, etal.

INTRODUCTION

Ah! These antinomies cause me great concern, because they confuse me. Praise God! These antinomies comfort me, because they assure me of God's control.

Antinomy, according to *Webster's New Collegiate Dictionary*, "a contradiction between two apparently equally valid principles or between inferences correctly drawn from such principles. Conflict (as of principles, ideas, or aspirations) insoluble in the light of available knowledge."

A synonym for antinomy is paradox. I picture it like this: a railroad track has two rails. These rails run parallel to each other, never merging, but both necessary. If one of the rails is missing the train, at best, is stalled or, at worst, wrecked.

> How do we balance election and free moral agency?

Theology as revealed in the Bible has antinomies. For example, God's ordained will and human responsibility is an antinomy.

Jesus was designated by God to die on the cross, but people, including you and me, are still held responsible for His death

Consider the antinomy in Simon Peter's sermon on the Day of Pentecost: "Men of Israel, listen to these words: This Jesus the Nazarene was a man pointed out to you by God with miracles, wonders, and signs that God did among you through Him, just as you yourselves know. Though He was delivered up according to God's determined plan and foreknowledge, you used lawless people to nail Him to a cross and kill Him." (Acts 2: 22-23).

The HCSB note is helpful: "Peter's declaration articulates a major paradox of the Christian life: Jesus' death occurred as a result of the plan and foreknowledge of God, but it was the free and sinful acts of human beings that executed that plan. The Bible often affirms the reality of both divine sovereignty and genuine human choice without explaining how the two can possibly work together without conflict."

Also, note Acts 4: 27-28: "For, in fact, in this city both Herod and Pontius Pilate, with the Gentiles and the people of Israel, assembled together against Your holy Servant Jesus, whom You anointed, to do whatever Your hand and Your plan had predestined to take place." Once again, we see divine sovereignty and human responsibility. Just because I cannot explain it doesn't mean it is not a valid theological concept. God's ways are not our ways, and His thoughts are not our thoughts. The heavens are high above us, and so are God's ways and thoughts far beyond us. We best fulfill our responsibility and leave sovereignty to God.

Joseph assured his guilty brothers that though they intended to do him harm, God had meant their deed for good: "And now don't be worried or angry with yourselves for selling me here, because God sent me ahead of you to preserve life. For the famine has been in the land these two years, and there will be five more years without plowing or harvesting. God sent me ahead of you to establish you as a remnant within the land and to keep you alive by a great deliverance. Therefore, it was not you who sent me here, but God..." (Genesis 45: 5-8a).

Again, from the HCSB note: "These verses stand as the theological high point of the account of Joseph's life (chaps 37-50) and one of the most eloquent affirmations in the Bible regarding God's sovereignty in human events." God sent Joseph to Egypt, but Joseph's brothers were still accountable for their sinful act in selling him as a slave.

There are many such antinomies in the Bible, but I want to

emphasize only two more: No one can come to Jesus for salvation except God the Father draws him: "No one can come to Me unless the Father who sent Me draws him, and I will raise him up at the last day." (John 6: 44). Yet, "whosoever will may come" (See John 7: 37: "On the last and most important day of the festival, Jesus stood up and cried out, 'If anyone is thirsty, he should come to Me and drink! The one who believes in Me, as the Scripture has said, will have streams of living water flow from deep with him.'"; See also Revelation 22: 17). Here we see two rails, side-by-side: only those God draws will come, but every person is responsible to come or suffer the consequences (hell) for not coming.

Again, it is said that William Carey, the "father of modern missions," stood before a group of pastors and appealed for them to send him to India to convert the heathen. One of those pastors reportedly told him, "Sit down, young man, when God gets ready to convert the heathen, He will do it in His own time and His own way." The man was right, but he forgot God's time—"Working together with Him, we also appeal to you, "Don't receive God's grace in vain." For He says: **I heard you in an acceptable time, and I helped you in the day of salvation.** Look, now is the acceptable time; now is the day of salvation." (2 Corinthians 6:1-2). He also forgot God's way— "Then Jesus came near and said to them, "All authority has been given to Me in heaven and on earth. Go, therefore, and make disciples of all nations, baptizing them in the name of the Father and of the Son and of the Holy Spirit, teaching them to observe everything I have commanded you. And remember, I am with you always, to the end of the age." (Matthew. 28: 18-20).

When one of the rails of God's sovereignty and human responsibility is forgotten, eliminated or over-emphasized, the gospel train is disabled. I have seen pastors kill churches by over-emphasizing God's sovereignty, and I have seen churches become immobile by under-emphasizing human responsibility (the responsibility of each individual to believe on the Lord Jesus Christ, and the responsibility for each born-again believer to share the gospel with those around him). That is why God ordained the plan of evangelism.

During the late 1970's and early 1980's I was privileged to lead many teams to South Korea on evangelism trips. We would enlist teams of three (a preacher, a musician, and a person to share his/her testimony) to go to South Korea. My dear friend, now with the Lord, Kim Soon Myung, an evangelist after my own heart, would go before us and schedule the churches and schools where we were to minister. I also worked in cooperation with Billy Kim, "the South Korean Billy Graham," in many crusades.

Kim Soon Myung was my personal interpreter. People testified that when he and I preached together it was if there was only one preacher. His personality and style so fit mine that we were used greatly by the Lord in evangelism. He set up crusades in super large churches of the original Christian denomination in South Korea. This denomination was extremely good at teaching the Bible to the South Koreans. In fact, many of the churches or schools that they sponsored ran more than 20,000 in attendance. However, this denomination used only one rail—they were hyper-Calvinists—teaching the truths of the scriptures, but never offering an opportunity to make an open decision for Jesus Christ (never giving an invitation).

Imagine the white harvest we found in these churches/schools! Over a period of a decade we made many trips to South Korea preaching the other rail—"whosoever will, may come," while keeping before us that only God can draw them. We recorded over 500,000 decisions for Christ during those crusades.

> "Sit down, young man! When God is ready to save the lost, He will do it in His own time and in His own way."

Perhaps one of the most dynamic illustrations of God's work through our teams was a young man who had surrendered to preach but had never preached a sermon publicly. On this particular trip we had enlisted more churches than preachers. So, we went to him and told him he had to preach. It scared the living daylights out of him, but he agreed to place himself in the hands of God and trust Him to do His work. We met with him and helped him organize a presentation of the gospel. Nervously, he shared the gospel and gave an invitation to accept Christ as Lord and Savior. To his great surprise there were more than 140 people who made public decisions for Christ. He was spoiled forever, like a fisherman who catches a prize trout on his first fishing expedition.

We gathered as a team for reports. There was much rejoicing—rejoicing from being overwhelmed at God's power—over each team's report. However, when he gave his report there was a standing ovation to the Lord for His goodness in using this first sermon for His glory.

My conclusion from these crusades and the circumstances was that I must always keep the two rails before me—no one comes to the Lord unless the Father draws him, and, yet, whosever will, may come. I have trained many young preachers and evangelists in my years of working with the North American Mission Board as an evangelism consultant, training pastors in third world countries, and teaching a class at California Baptist University for a number of years. I have always told them to recognize the two rails and enjoy the ride.

Just for the record, we published my follow-up materials, *How to Know and Grow in Christ*, in the Korean language lest we leave these people without direction. Also, remember that they were mostly already related to a local church, either through attendance or through the schools that the churches sponsored. We have always tried to be complete evangelists—winning people to Christ, leading them to be baptized into the local church, teaching them God's Word, and training them as God's disciples.

"The people that walked in darkness have seen a great light." That was the message of the prophet Isaiah (chap. 9, verse 2), which he gave over half a century before Jesus came to the earth. Sin is a darkness which causes frustration, fear, doubt, immorality, lawlessness, and a thousand other ills. People caught in darkness seek a light...a light to show them the way. Such a Light has shone..." I am the Light of the world" (Jesus in John 8: 12) ...but the saddest fact of all is the people didn't recognize Him as that Light...the Light that illuminates all who put their trust in Him as Lord and Savior. "This is the condemnation that light has come into the world, but men loved darkness rather than light, because their deeds were evil" (John 3)—author unknown.

Evangelism is telling forth the "good news" to the people who are in darkness. In Jesus' day the kings led their battle troops out to war against the enemy. The people of his kingdom awaited news concerning the conflict...they were "in the dark" as to what was the welfare of their loved ones and the outcome of the battle. Then when the battle was over there was sent a runner, an evangelist, to tell the good news, the evangel, to the people who "sat in darkness." Like in Ezekiel, the question came, "Watchman, what of the night?" The watchman bore the good news that dawn was coming and there was no danger...in this case the evangelist bore the good news that the victory had been won...the Light had come.

Evangelism is answering Jesus' question to His disciples, "Who do men say that I the Son of Man am? We cannot be satisfied with "some say this, and some say that." We have to give a sure answer—the answer that Simon Peter gave as it was revealed to him: "You are the Christ the Son of the Living God". It was Nicodemus' problem—he didn't have the right answer, considering Jesus to be only a good teacher sent from God. This was the point of his need of repentance—to properly recognize who Jesus was and is. He was a good man, but still lost because he did not have the right opinion of Jesus as Lord and Savior.

As indicated in the text, many answers come from the world, every one of them wrong. The only correct answer is to point people to the substitutionary and sacrificial death of Jesus upon the cross and the resurrection from the dead, the necessity of repentance from sin, and placing one's faith in Jesus Christ as Lord and Savior. Please notice the order that I gave—the order that I got from Scripture. One cannot receive Jesus as Savior and make Him Lord later on. He receives Him as Lord and He becomes Savior—the "He" is Jesus Christ the Son of the Living God.

In this work I am going to give you several headings: the biblical basis for evangelism, a general overview of the principles of evangelism, who, why, what, when, where, and how to do evangelism, the characteristics of the evangelist (the personal witness), the mechanics of presenting the gospel effectively, and how to give a good invitation.

If we are to give good public invitations, we need to know what we are inviting them to. That is why I included a section on the biblical basis for evangelism, intentional evangelism, basic principles, soteriology, and the personal worker (See next paragraph). We can learn this through becoming skilled in personal and private invitations.

> Giving good public invitations is learned by giving good private invitations.

The reason I have included sections on the biblical basis for evangelism and training for the personal worker in doing personal evangelism is to give a fuller picture that precedes the invitation. This training has been given to thousands of counselors that worked in the crusades we led (Incidentally, we have seen many people come to Christ during our counselor training, even a handful of pastors). These methods are tried and proven to be effective in reaching people with the gospel of Jesus Christ.

There is so much more that I wanted to share about evangelism, but space did not permit. Perhaps, at a future date God will lead me to write more on the subject.

May His name be praised and may you and I together take along with us many people as we enter into His presence. May He bless you as you apply these ideas to the ministry, He has committed to you.

In this book I use "disciple winner" interchangeably with "soul-winner" (Actually, there is only one soul-winner in the universe, namely, the Holy Spirit). I feel the best term is "witnessing". To me evangelism is sharing the gospel of Jesus Christ in the power of the Holy Spirit, giving people an honest opportunity to respond, and leaving the results in the hands of God.

My prayer is that this book will enlighten, encourage, and strengthen you in your efforts when witnessing to the saving power of Jesus Christ. I urge you and me to be unashamed of the gospel, for it is the power of God unto salvation to everyone that believes.

THE BIBLICAL BASIS FOR EVANGELISM

What is the basis upon which I make my arguments for intentional evangelism and the gospel invitation? The biblical basis for evangelism may be given by alliterating six "M's". They are as follows:

THE MEANING OF EVANGELISM (SIGNIFICATION).

Evangelism is our **means of origin** (Jesus Christ came into the world to save sinners of whom I am chief). It is also our **means of growth**. The church grows when evangelism is practiced. It declines when evangelism is neglected (paraphrased from Roland Q. Leavell). The largest number of baptisms my denomination has ever recorded was during 1955. Why did that happen? Because we used the major tool of evangelism available to us known as what we call "Sunday School" (Actually, I mean Bible study. I have planted churches where I had no classroom space for Sunday School, but had small groups in all kinds of places—homes, restaurants, work-places, etc.). My denomination had a campaign in 1954 called "A Million More in Fifty-four." During 1954 we enrolled more than a million new students in our Sunday Schools. The result was, that in the next year (1955), we had the largest number of baptisms we have ever recorded in any one year.

Consider that for a moment! With all of our new methods, all of our technology (radio, TV, Internet, etc.) we still had more baptisms than any other year, because we did the basics of enrolling people in Bible study groups ("Faith comes by hearing and hearing by the Word of God"). Does not this speak to you of the importance of working with individuals, even in small groups, in order to spread the gospel?

Evangelism is our only **means of perpetuity**. The history of Christianity is strewn with the records of churches that were once great, but now dead—dead spiritually or dead as to existence, because they stopped doing evangelism and became centro-focused. If this generation does not evangelize then there will be no Christianity in the next generation. If we do not have evangelism at the forefront, we have no biblical basis for existence. We become social clubs instead of a marching army in the cause of Christ. Evangelism has its base in the Bible. While the value of church property, church membership, and total gifts have sky-rocketed, our number of baptisms has remained almost static to the point that we know that somebody (somebodies) is not doing his job in evangelism. Origin, growth, and perpetuity are so ingrained in the New Testament methods of evangelism that whoever denies, ignores, neglects, or spurns these three endangers any established work or any proposed new work.

Dr. Roland Q. Leavell wrote, "The Great Commission is the MAGNA CHARTA of evangelism. It is the marching orders of the supreme Commander. It is the proclamation of the King of kings to all His kingdom citizens. It is Christ's imperative for all who name His name.

> **Evangelism**:
>
> our means of origin, growth and, perpetuity.
>
> The Magna Charta of the Church

"In this commission there is one dominant and controlling imperative, while all the other verb forms are participles. The imperative is "make disciples." The word that is translated "go" is a participle and could be translated "going" or "as you go." Likewise, the words translated "baptizing" and "teaching" are participles. While these participles are immensely important, the imperative "make disciples" is of superlative importance. That means that soul-winning is central, that evangelism is the divine imperative, that world-wide endeavor is the very heart of Christ's commands to His disciples.

"Evangelism has its compelling urge within a burning, loving heart. The lack of compassion for souls is the greatest tragedy of Christians and of churches through the world. Many Christians wish for another Pentecost. Pentecostal success will never come without Pentecostal prayer, Pentecostal passion for souls, Pentecostal personal witnessing, Pentecostal preaching. Great Pentecostal experiences can and do come to those whose minds and hearts are saturated with the message and meaning of the Word of God."

A DESCRIPTION OF EVANGELISM

Here is my description of evangelism based on Matthew 28: 18-20 (I attempt to describe it rather than define it, because it is more easily described than defined). I will use a sandwich to describe it, using a chart:

1st slice of bread   HIS POWER

Meat	Winning people to Christ
Lettuce	Baptizing people in His Name
Tomato	Teaching people God's Word
Relish	Training people in His skills (note: these four things could easily be interchanged—all are important).

2nd slice of bread   His Presence

Note: The bread is what holds the sandwich together. It is His power and His presence that makes our task possible. **That power and that presence are promised only to those who do the work of**

the Great Commission.

What is evangelism? Evangelism is to herald a message of importance. Much that is referred to as evangelism is not. A definition of evangelism is: "To present Christ in the power of the Holy Spirit, so that men shall come to put their trust in God, accepting Him as Lord and seek to serve Him in the fellowship of His church."

What is personal evangelism? It is seeking to reach the person beside you as Andrew brought his brother, Peter, to Jesus (John 1: 35ff.). You never know who you will win. Lesser men bring greater. Andrew brought Peter. Edward Kimball, a shoe salesman brought D. L. Moody. Jimmy Warren brought Rick Warren.

THE MOTIVATION FOR EVANGELISM (STIMULATION)

MOTIVES FOR EVANGELISM

How often the New Testament talks about evangelism
Actions of the New Testament characters
Command of our Lord
Our own experience is worth sharing
Needs of the world
Fate of people without Christ
Things people miss without Christ
Concern for the needs of others
Work of the Holy Spirit

To be evangelistic we need some strong motives. It does not come from within us. A church always tends to drift away from evangelism and never towards it. **We are motivated because of how much the New Testament talks about evangelism**. The word for evangel or gospel appears 103 times in the New Testament. As I have already written, the word for evangel is used outside the New Testament to refer to a runner who was returning from the battlefield to bring the good news to the home people that the army had conquered its foe, that it had been victorious. The people could tell what the message was by the way he ran. (Can they tell our message by the way we live?) A young lady said to me, "When I was around Mrs. _____ I felt that she had something I didn't have, and I very badly wanted it."

We are motivated by the actions of the men of the Bible in evangelism. First, Jesus was so involved in evangelism that He had very little time to rest. In Matthew 8 this can be seen. He heals the leper, then the centurion's servant, and Peter's mother-in-law. Then when it was evening, He thought to rest, but they brought to Him many that were possessed with devils and He cast the devils out. Someone immediately argues that this has to do with physical ministry upon the part of our Lord. That is true, but you never find Him meeting someone's physical need without at the same time trying to meet their spiritual need (2 Corinthians 5 depicts us doing the ministry of reconciliation and giving the message of reconciliation). In the Scripture there is the Divine example of Jesus (Luke 19: 10: "For the Son of Man has come to seek and to save that which was lost." John 9: 4: "We must do the works of Him who sent Me while it is day. Night is coming when no one can work.") In these two passages we find both the mission and the urgency of Christ's ministry on earth. When a person meets Christ, he learns to love souls.

Jesus made every manner of personal contact in soul-winning. He sought to win Pharisees, Sadducees, Herodians, and Zealots. He interviewed rulers of the Sanhedrin, Samaritans, Galileans, Greeks, Romans, and other Gentiles. His incessant disciple-winning led Him to deal with common people, wise men, publicans, harlots, lechers, little children, soldiers, thieves, beggars, fishermen, tax gatherers, and lovely women.

He sought to win disciples under all manner of circumstances. He won several disciples while they were fishing. Matthew was won while collecting taxes. A woman was won at Jacob's well. A lawyer was won while on the highway; another was won in a Pharisee's house; Zaccheus was won while on the street; the dying thief was won while on the cross.

He used every method of evangelism, becoming all things to all men that by all means they might be saved. He capitalized on His social engagements, and He utilized the quietness of private conferences. He preached with mighty power, and He taught God's truth to all who would learn of Him. He rebuked hypocrisy, He wept over the wavering.

Second, Paul was deeply involved in evangelism. Seventy-seven times that the word evangel or gospel is used in the New Testament they appear in relation to Paul. He lived and breathed evangelism. If you take when Paul was saved, subtract the time he was in jail, and the time he was in the desert, you will find that he had only 15-20 years of service in public ministry. Yet, look what he did without modern means (no radio, no phone, no television, no rapid transportation, no internet, no computer, etc.). He literally disturbed his world.

Third, other early Christians are examples of evangelism. John the Baptist's example is worthy of emulation, for "the two disciples heard him speak, and they followed Jesus" (John 1: 37). Andrew brought his brother to Christ (John 1: 40-42). Like many disciple-winners since that time, Andrew brought to Christ a man more capable than himself. Andrew also introduced some Greeks to the Lord (John 12: 21-23). Philip brought Nathaniel (John1: 43-46); Stephen died while witnessing to those who killed him (Acts7); Barnabas gave himself to God in disciple-winning.

We are motivated by the command of our Lord. We do not evangelize because we want to, nor because we plan or desire to, but because we are under orders to do so. Disobedience to this command is to destroy the church. We evangelize because of the AUTHORITY OF THE SCRIPTURES. "Do the work of an evangelist" (2 Timothy 4: 5) is the authoritative command of the scriptures. In the scripture there is the commission of Christ to His disciples to evangelize.

Two quotations need to be linked together: "For the Son of Man has come to seek and to save that which is lost (Luke. 19:10), and "As My Father has sent Me, even so I send you" (John 20: 21). Jesus promised power to those who would carry out these commands and be disciple-winners. He promised His presence to those who would be faithful in witnessing (Acts 1: 8). He promised to direct us to where and why, to what and to whom we should bear witness. The early disciples took disciple-winning as a serious matter (Acts 4: 1-20). Do we?

Paul declares us to be "ambassadors for Christ" (2 Corinthians. 5: 20). Ambassadors for Christ grossly misrepresent their Sovereign if they do not love souls, yearn for souls, plead with souls, and if necessary, even die for souls. Ambassadors don't make up the message; they share the message of their Sovereign.

Our experience motivates us. We will not evangelize without the sense of Christ in our hearts. When you meet Christ, a whole new focal point comes. A new relationship: not just a horizontal relationship, but also a vertical relationship. We cease to be introverts and become extroverts for Christ. Because the vertical relationship is changed, the horizontal relationship is also changed. We are brought together by the centripetal force of Jesus Christ in the church, and we are sent out by the centrifugal force of evangelism by the Holy Spirit. The sign at the entrance to my church is two-sided: as one enters, he reads, "Welcome to worship." As he leaves the parking lot, he reads, "You are now entering the mission field."

Our early experience with Him is most dynamic. The best time to get a person to adopt new attitudes, new responsibilities, is when he first comes into this relationship. Do you remember how excited you were to tell someone else of your new relationship with Jesus when you were first saved? Is it possible we have become like the Church of Laodicea, losing our first love? If so, take the counsel of God and get back your first love. Three things are prescribed to get back to our first love: remember from what you have fallen; repent of what you are doing wrong or neglecting; and, redo what you did at the first (See Revelation 3: 16-22).

We are motivated by the needs of our world. War and strife and pagan ideologies have brought the world into a time of unprecedented revenge, hatred, and strife. Materialism is the philosophy of multitudes, and the god of gold is the god of millions of people. Greed, gambling, illicit sex, dope, and godless pursuit after material things indicate a dearth of concern for spiritual things. Terrorism ransacks our world today. The Christian of today needs to pray with Habakkuk of old, "O Jehovah, revive thy work in the midst of years" (Habakkuk 3:2).

The world is DEGRADED BY SIN. Read the first chapter of Romans and you will see how degrading sin really is. People run rampantly after evil. Worse, they are not content to do evil themselves; they want to involve others with them.

The world is CRITICALLY IN NEED OF CHRIST. From one-half to three-fifths of the world's people are without a preacher, a teacher, or a doctor. The pagan population of the world is increasing annually about six to ten million faster that Christians are winning pagan people to Christ. The pagans are not all in foreign countries; many of them are right where we live.

New foes of Christianity, including a hostile government, have arisen. Terrorism resulting from radicals of those opposed to Christ has murdered hundreds of thousands. Martyrdom, (physical, emotional and psychological), is rampant in the whole world. Communism, nationalism, atheism, materialism, and humanism take their toll on the Christian endeavor.

Half or more of the people of the United States have no religious affiliation whatever, and millions without Christian affiliation. There are 10,000 plus villages in the United States without a church, 30,000 plus villages and towns without a resident pastor, and at least 14,000,000 children who are receiving no religious education. Many within the churches have a form of godliness without the power of it. Sin-sickness today is soul-deep, fever-hot, and critical.

The awful fate of people who do not know Christ motivates us. One one-minute look into hell would change our concerns. Hell is real—Jesus said much more about hell than heaven (I picture Jesus talking about hell with a tear in his eye). People without Jesus Christ go to hell. I don't want my family or friends to go to hell. I don't want my enemies to go to hell. Are you skeptical about hell? Then you don't believe Jesus. A man once told Billy Sunday he did not believe for one moment there was a place called hell. Billy replied, "You won't be there five minutes before you change your mind."

Hell is an awful place—a place of torment, bickering and fighting, a place where people continue sinning, becoming worse and worse, and a place of no escape (See Luke 19 where it indicates that people there blame God for not giving them enough evidence). It is a place with awful company (Revelation. 21: 8; Matthew. 25: 41).

The things people will miss if they don't know Christ motivates us. They miss a joyous, fruitful, peaceful and blessed life in this world, and the joys of heaven, a land of no tears, no dying, no sorrow, and no pain, in the future world. They miss the wonderful company of the heavenly residents such as the patriarchs, disciples, prophets, family and friends. Most of all, they miss Jesus.

We are motivated because the Christian should be concerned for lost souls. Spurgeon once wrote, "The surest sign a slave has been set free is that he wants to set other slaves free as well." The Scriptures emphasize the LOSTNESS OF PEOPLE without Jesus Christ. Study the word pictures of lostness in Luke 15 (lost to direction as the sheep, lost to worth as the coin, lost to purpose as the younger son, and lost by attitude as the older son). Also, study lostness by such Scriptures as 1 Peter 3: 19; 2 Peter 2: 4, 19; Luke 16: 23, 24). These passages should bring a concern for those who are lost. Evangelism will abound wherever and whenever Christians see people as Christ saw them—lost, scattered as sheep without a shepherd, despairing, defeated, doomed, dying, and damned. Christ's love for the lost made Him the supreme disciple-winner. It will do the same for his followers.

If a person is spiritually healthy, he will have a compassion for souls. Look again at the normal Christian activity in the life of Andrew and Philip (John 1: 41-45). The trouble with most unhappy and unfruitful Christians is that they are living a sub-normal Christian life. A revival is not an abnormal time, but, rather, it is a time when Christians are brought up to the normal activity of Christianity as described in the Bible. There is normal victory and normal happiness, which should prevail perennially.

We are motivated by the work of the Holy Spirit. An inner compulsion comes when the Holy Spirit comes. There were three things present in the beginning of the church: (1) the people were together in prayer; (2) the Holy Spirit came upon them in power; and, (3) they went out to witness. This is always happening in the beginning of new work. It will be true if the work continues in vitality. No wonder Paul said, "Woe is me if I preach not the gospel." If you are looking for a formula for revival in your life or in your church, there it is—meet together in soul-searching prayer, expect the Holy Spirit to get involved with you, and, then, go out and spread the gospel. You will see revival come.

1. Here is a list of V. L. Stanfield's motives as given in his lectures:
   a. By thinking about what Christ has done for us.
   b. By thinking about what Christ has done for others.
   c. By the command of our Lord.
   d. Love of Christ.
   e. Man's need for fellowship with God.
   f. What men who don't know Christ face—death, judgment, and hell.
   g. What comes to men in Christ—life, joy, peace, purpose, and Heaven.
   h. What Christ can do for our homes.
   i. What Christian faith does for society.
   j. The church needs men and women—Lord's army needs soldiers.
   k. What it will do for the life of a church.
   l. What will happen to us if we do or don't spread the gospel.
   m. Irresistible desire is the highest motive.

2. Here is George Sweazey's list of motives.
   a. God's intention for human life.
   b. Jesus' clear commandment.
   c. The situation in our communities.
   d. Sin and the solution.
   e. Homes—what it will do for them.
   f. Need for practical guidance for people.
   g. Power to overcome temptation.
   h. God's help in time of trouble.
   i. Purpose for living.
   j. Loyalties—Christ gives a person something to cling to.
   k. Social righteousness.
   l. Overcome death.
   m. People's need of the church.
   n. The church's need of people.
   o. Our own soul's good.

3. Here is Jesse M. Bader's list of motives.
   a. Compulsions from without—the command of Christ and the need of America
   b. The need of the church.

c. The story is told of two men who were lost in a blinding snowstorm in Canada. The temperature was well below zero. Both men became numb from the cold. One of them, more helpless than the other, finally gave up and lay down in the snow to die. His friend did his best to save him. Though he was numb with the cold himself, he began to slap and rub the body of his friend. He got him on his feet and walked him about. It was not long before the man's body began to respond and warm up. He continued working until his friend was fully restored. Suddenly the man realized that by putting the warmth into the body of his companion, he had put warmth into his own body. So, we find that when we seek to bring others to Christ, we bring ourselves to Him.

THE MESSAGE OF EVANGELISM (Stating the gospel)

In the first chapter of John, verses 1-3 and in verse 14, we see the message of evangelism summed up in five statement: 1) God in the person of Jesus Christ placed Himself into the human struggle in history; 2) God in the person of Jesus Christ created human perfection in order to show us how we ought to live; 3) God in the person of Jesus Christ made atonement for our sin; 4) God conquered death in the risen Christ; and, 5) God initiated a new order, a new community—a colony of heaven on earth—the Christian church, by His Holy Spirit. Jesse Bader wrote, "The gospel is good news about something God did in history and something He becomes in history, in Jesus Christ."

The early ministers of Disciples of Christ presented the gospel of Christ to those not members of any church in three divisions: 1) FACTS to be believed; 2) COMMANDS to be obeyed; and, 3) PROMISES to be enjoyed. The facts to be believed were the incarnation, the crucifixion, and the resurrection of Christ. The commands to be obeyed were faith, repentance and baptism. The promises to be enjoyed were forgiveness of sin, the gift of the Holy Spirit and eternal life.

Jesse Bader pointed out that "...on Calvary's hill there were three crosses. On one cross died a man in sin. On the opposite cross died a man to sin, and on the center, cross died a man for sin." I have a sermon using that outline.

Whatever the people asked Jesus for He gave them, except He wouldn't give signs, saying that we must come by faith. They asked for bread and He gave it to them. They asked for health and He gave it to them. They asked for truth and He gave it to them. They asked for His life and He gave that also.

Again, I refer you to Bader who tells us of the tremendous dimensions of the cross. Let me quote him: "How long is it? It is as broad as the human race. It includes every person. How deep down does it go? It goes down to the deepest sorrow, suffering and sin. How high is it? It is as high as man's holiest thought. It reaches up to the throne of God."

Our message is not in the incarnation and the cross only. The men of the New Testament always pointed men to the incarnation to show that He was God—pointed people to the cross to show that in love He died for man—and pointed to the resurrection to show that God conquered death, and because He died and arose, we can be raised too—and pointed to His second coming as our final victory.

There is plenty of proof of His resurrection. (a) From the day of His resurrection to the day of His ascension He appeared at least eleven times. (b) More than six hundred (600) persons saw Him in His varied appearances. (c) The disciples witnessed boldly to His resurrection. It is extremely doubtful they would have died for Him had they doubted that He lived. As James S. Stewart has said, "The resurrection of Christ from the dead is no appendix to the faith. This is the faith...The Lord has risen indeed!"

SOTERIOLOGY

The message of evangelism is summed up by the use of a number of terms. I will now give a summary of these terms as compiled from Louis Sperry Chafer, H. L. Wilmington and E. Y. Mullins. I would recommend a sermon (bible study) series on these terms. The Bible will be the only illustration material you will need in presenting these messages. Following then is the list of terms (See the paragraph following: I, C, 4) that give at least a near-complete, if not complete, description of the message of the evangelists. Theologians call this doctrine "**soteriology**."

> **MESSAGE IN**
> **12 WORDS**
> *Redemption*
> *Reconciliation*
> *Propitiation*
> *Conversion*
> *Repentance*
> *Faith*
> *Regeneration*
> *Forgiveness*
> *Justification*
> *Sanctification*
> *Preservation*
> *Glorification*

The Meaning of Soteriology

1. "Soteriology is that portion of Systematic Theology that treats the subject of salvation. The word *salvation* is a translation of the Greek word *soteria*, which is derived from the Greek word *soter,* which means *Savior*" (Chafer).

2. Let's look at the word as it is used in the Old Testament. It was used in the Old Testament as meaning "deliverance," such as when Israel was delivered from Egyptian bondage, or when delivered from Babylonian bondage.

a. This is more involved because of what we call "progressive revelation."

b. Christ alluded to "progressive revelation" when He said, "First the blade, then the ear, after that the full corn in the ear" (Mark 4: 28).

Note: I will only deal with this subject as displayed in the New Testament. For a fuller explanation, read from Chafer, Mullins and Wilmington.

3. Let's look at soteriology in the New Testament.

a. The New Testament Age is distinguished in that there is now no difference between Jew and Gentile either with regard to their lost estate or their need of salvation by grace (Romans 3: 9). What then? Are we any better?[a] Not at all! For we have previously charged that both Jews and Gentiles[b] are all under sin,…"

b. There is also no difference with regard to terms upon which they can be saved (Romans 10: 11). Now the Scripture says, everyone who believes on Him will not be put to shame…"

c. Regarding the terms such as deliverance, safety, preservation, soundness, restoration, and healing as used in the Old Testament, it is important to note that in the New Testament the major emphasis is on the work of God on the behalf of mankind.

d. This is the one most comprehensive doctrine in the Bible. It can be summarized under 12 words representing vital doctrines, all of which need consideration: redemption, reconciliation, propitiation, conversion, repentance, faith, regeneration, forgiveness, justification, sanctification, preservation, and glorification. We will give a cursory look at each of these terms.

REDEMPTION:

Luke 1: 68: Praise the Lord, the God of Israel, because He has visited and provided redemption for His people.

3 meanings of redemption:

1) to pay a ransom price for something or someone: (Hebrews 9: 12) He entered the most holy place once for all, not by the blood of goats and calves, but by His own blood, having obtained eternal redemption.

2) to remove from a slave marketplace (Galatians 3: 13) Christ has redeemed us from the curse of the law by becoming a curse for us, because it is written: Everyone who is hung on a tree is cursed.[a]

REDEMPTION

To pay a price for something or someone

To redeem from the market place

To affect a full release and place in the family by adoption

---

3) to affect a full release (Romans 8: 22-23) For we know that the whole creation has been groaning together with labor pains until now. And not only that, be we ourselves who have the Spirt as the firstfruits—we also groan within ourselves, eagerly waiting for adoption, the redemption of our bodies.

The cost of redemption (1 Peter 1: 18-19) [18] For you know that you were redeemed from your empty way of life inherited from the fathers, not with perishable things like silver or gold, [19] but with the precious blood of Christ, like that of a lamb without defect or blemish.

Redemption can be wonderfully illustrated from either Hosea who bought back his wife from the slave market, or from the Book of Ruth as it describes the GOEL, kinsman-redeemer. The kinsman-redeemer had to have three major qualities: first, he had to be next of kin—Jesus became next of kin to us by His incarnation, being tempted in all points as we are, yet without sin; second, he had to be willing to redeem us—Jesus' willingness being shown by His death upon the cross; and, third, he had to be able to redeem—"Therefore, He is always able to save those who come to God through Him, since He always lives to intercede for them." (Hebrews 7: 25: along with many other passages).

> "You are not your own." Though precious enough to have been bought with a price, yet none of the preciousness is yours. Believers, you are the goods and chattels of Christ. As you were once sold under sin, so are you now "bought with a price." Never can the fact of our immersion into the sacred name be reversed. Only once and that to last forever, we are buried with Christ in baptism unto death. Into His name have we been plunged, that we may be His forever and no more our own. A man cannot be proud of himself, however he knows his value, when He perceives that not a hair on his head or a finger of his hands belongs to himself.[2] – Charles Spurgeon

RECONCILIATION:

2 Corinthians 5: 19: [19] That is, in Christ, God was reconciling the world to Himself, not counting their trespasses against them, and He has committed the message of reconciliation to us.

2 meanings:1) Old Testament: to cover something, usually translated "Atonement".

2) New Testament: to change from an enemy to a friend (Ephesians 2: 16). [16] He did this so that He might reconcile both to God in one body through the cross and put the hostility to death by it.[3]

---

[2] Charles Spurgeon, Redemption by Price, Sermon #1554, Public Domain, spurgeongems.org/vols25-27/chs1554.pdf, P. 5.

3) 2 phases: one, God has reconciled Himself to the world through Christ (2 Corinthians 5: 18-19) [18] Everything is from God, who reconciled us to Himself through Christ and gave us the ministry of reconciliation: [19] That is, in Christ, God was reconciling the world to Himself, not counting their trespasses against them, and He has committed the message of reconciliation to us.; and, two, Man is now to reconcile himself to God through Christ (2 Corinthians 5: 20). Therefore, we are ambassadors for Christ, certain that God is appealing through us. We plead on Christ's behalf, "Be reconciled to God."

> **RECONCILIATION**
>
> *To cover something:*
> *usually translated*
> *"Atonement."*
> *To change from an*
> *enemy to a friend.*
> *God has reconciled*
> *Himself to us by the death*
> *of His Son.*
> *We must now reconcile*
> *ourselves to God through*
> *faith in Jesus Christ.*

For a great Bible illustration of reconciliation see the story of Joseph reconciling himself to his brothers, pointing out that they were never fully able to reconcile themselves to Joseph. Emphasize that reconciliation is a two-way street.

Note: My wife and I have a series of three books on reconciliation, including 6 messages (Book one), 6 Bible study lessons (Book two), and a 40-day devotional book (Book three). The pastors need Book one; the Bible study teachers need Book two (perhaps the class members should also have this book); and, all of the people need Book three since they are asked to read one devotional on reconciliation for forty days, the devotionals covering all kinds of reconciliation.

PROPITIATION:

1 John 2: 2: He Himself is the propitiation for our sins, and not only for ours, but also for those of the whole world. 1 John 4: 10: Love consists in this: not that we loved God, but that He loved us and sent His Son to be the[a] propitiation for our sins.

1) The meaning is to render favorable, to appease or to satisfy.

2) The method is Romans 3: 25; [25] God presented Him as a propitiation[a] through faith in His blood, to demonstrate His righteousness, because in His restraint God passed over the sins previously committed." Ephesians 2: 13. But now in Christ Jesus, you who were far away have been brought near by the blood of the Messiah."

PROPITIATION

MEANING: to render favorable; to satisfy

METHOD: the death of Jesus

NECESSITY: God's wrath

PLACE: OT—Mercy Seat; NT—Cross

RESULT: God is justified in forgiving sin and in bestowing righteousness

---

3) The necessity is because of God's wrath (John 3: 36: The one who believes in the Son has eternal life, but the one who refuses to believe in the Son will not see life; instead, the wrath of God remains on him.; Romans 1: 18: For God's wrath is revealed from heaven against all godlessness and unrighteousness of people who by their unrighteousness suppress the truth.)

4) The place: in the Old Testament it was the mercy seat (Exodus 25: 22: I will meet with you there above the mercy seat, between the two cherubim that are over the ark of the testimony; I will speak with you from there about all that I command you regarding the Israelites.); in the New Testament it is at Golgotha (Calvary—the Cross) Romans 5: 10: For if, while we were enemies, we were reconciled to God through the death of His Son, then how much

more, having been reconciled, will we be saved by His life!.

5) The result: God is justified in forgiving sin; God is justified in bestowing righteousness (Romans 3: 25-26: God presented Him as a propitiation[a] through faith in His blood, to demonstrate His righteousness, because in His restraint God passed over the sins previously committed. [26] God presented Him to demonstrate His righteousness at the present time, so that He would be righteous and declare righteous[b] the one who has faith in Jesus.).

CONVERSION: Psalm 19: 7: The instruction of the LORD is perfect, renewing one's life (KJV, "converting the soul"); the testimony of the LORD is trustworthy, making the inexperienced wise.; Psalm 51: 13: [13] Then I will teach the rebellious Your ways, and sinners will return to You." ; Acts 3: 19: Therefore repent and turn back, so that your sins may be wiped out, that seasons of refreshing may come from the presence of the Lord,"[a] This word leads to the next two words: repentance and faith. For an illustration, you may wish to use the tormentor Saul who became the apostle Paul.

Keep in mind that conversion is only a turning. Unless it is mixed with faith and repentance, it leaves the person in the state of the hard ground, the thorny ground and the shallow ground. There must be advancement in the life of one who is converted to the other aspects of soteriology.

REPENTANCE:

Meaning of repentance: not reformation as seen in self-help programs; not remorse as seen in Judas or Esau (*metalomai*); not penitence as practiced by the Roman Catholics; it is a voluntary and sincere turning from sin—change of mind, emotion, will, and direction (*metonia*) (John 16: 7-11: Nevertheless, I am telling you the truth. It is for your benefit that I go away, because if I don't go away the Counselor will not come to you. If I go, I will send Him to you. [8] When He comes, He will convict the world about sin, righteousness, and judgment: [9] About sin, because they do not believe in Me; [10] about righteousness, because I am going to the Father and you will no longer see Me; [11] and about judgment, because the ruler of this world has been judged; Acts 17: 30: "Therefore, having overlooked the times of ignorance, God now commands all people everywhere to repent), (See the section on the "Invitation" to find some ideas for preaching repentance).

| About foot-logs, |
| repentance and faith |

FAITH:

Meaning of faith: not a blind leap into the dark, but an intelligent step into the light of God's promises; not speculation; it is a voluntary and sincere change of mind of the sinner causing him to turn to Christ for salvation. (Acts 20:21: I testified to both Jews and Greeks about repentance toward God and faith in our Lord Jesus.)

Illustration: As a boy I learned agility by walking a board fence as I fed the cattle. One day my dad and I were challenged to cross a stream that was cascading rapidly. There was a tree fallen across the stream upon which we could walk. I was unable to swim, but I assured my dad that, because I could walk the board fence, I could walk the "foot log". We started at the trunk end of the tree and I was doing fine for a while, but as the tree grew smaller and began to shake, the waters below were terrifying to me since I couldn't swim. As I felt I was beginning to fall, I spun around and grabbed hold of my dad, so he could hold me up. In that one turning, I expressed both repentance and faith—repentance of my childish pride and faith in my dad's ability to save me.

Likewise, all people need to repent of self-will and turn to Christ in faith that He can save

REGENERATION

MEANING: a process whereby God through a second birth imparts to the believing sinner a new nature

NECESSITY: man's sinful nature and actions

EXTENT: individually, a new person in Christ; universally, the removal of the curse

AGENTS: Word of God, Man of God, and Spirit of God

1) How do we get faith? (Romans 10: 17: So, faith comes from what is heard, and what is heard comes through the message about Christ). Their hearing is the responsibility of the evangelist.

2) Is it necessary? (Hebrews 11: 6: Now without faith it is impossible to please God, for the one who draws near to Him must believe that He exists and rewards those who seek Him; Ephesians 2: 8-9: For you are saved by grace through faith, and this is not from yourselves; it is God's gift— 9 not from works, so that no one can boast.).

REGENERATION:

(Titus 3: 5: 5 He saved us—not by works of righteousness that we had done, but according to His mercy, through the washing of regeneration and renewal by the Holy Spirit.).

1) The meaning is the process whereby God through a second birth imparts to the believing sinner a new nature (John 3: 3: And everyone who has this hope in Him purifies himself just as He is pure; John 1: 12-13: But to all who did receive Him, He gave them the right to be[a] children of God, to those who believe in His name, [13] who were born, not of blood,[b] or of the will of the flesh, or of the will of man,[c] but of God)."

This process does not come from parents ("born not of blood"), nor from human resolutions ("not of the will of the flesh"), nor from the decision of the church ("nor of the will of man"), but from God through the new birth.

2) The necessity of regeneration: (Jeremiah 13: 23: [23] Can the Cushite change his skin, or a leopard his spots? If so, you might be able to do what is good, you who are instructed in evil; Romans 3: 10-18: as it is written:[a]There is no one righteous, not even one.[11] There is no one who understands; there is no one who seeks God.[12] All have turned away; all alike have become useless. There is no one who does what is good, not even one.[b][13] Their throat is an open grave; they deceive with their tongues.[c]Vipers' venom is under their lips.[d][14] Their mouth is full of cursing and bitterness.[e][15] Their feet are swift to shed blood;[16] ruin and wretchedness are in their paths,[17] and the path of peace they have not known.[f][18] There is no fear of God before their eyes.[g])

    a. Dead to God (Ephesians 2: 1: And you were dead in your trespasses and sins).

    b. Children of wrath (Ephesians 2: 3: We too all previously lived among them in our fleshly desires, carrying out the inclinations of our flesh and thoughts, and we were by nature children under wrath as the others were also.)

    c. Sons of disobedience (Ephesians 2: 2: in which you previously walked according to the ways of this world, according to the ruler who exercises authority over the lower heavens,[a] the spirit now working in the disobedient.[)])

    d. Under a curse (Romans 5: 12: Therefore, just as sin entered the world through one man, and death through sin, in this way death spread to all men, because all sinned).

3) The extent: Individual (Titus 3:5: He saved us—not by works of righteousness that we had done, but according to His mercy, through the washing of regeneration and renewal by the Holy Spirit.).

There will be the universal—regeneration of nature (Romans 8: 19-23: [19] For the creation eagerly awaits with anticipation for God's sons to be revealed. [20] For the creation was subjected to futility—not willingly, but because of Him who subjected it—in the hope [21] that the creation itself will also be set free from the bondage of corruption into the glorious freedom of God's children. [22] For we know that the whole creation has been groaning together with labor pains until now. [23] And not only that, but we ourselves who have the Spirit as the firstfruits—we also groan within ourselves, eagerly waiting for adoption, the redemption of our bodies.)

There will also be the individual regeneration of the believer. I illustrate this by using the incident between Jesus and Nicodemus, pointing out that Nicodemus had to change his mind about who Jesus was (repentance), and be born again as Jesus described it: a change that can be evidenced but not seen (the wind).

4) Three agents in regeneration: *The Word of God* (John 3: 5: Jesus answered, "I assure you: Unless someone is born of water and the Spirit,[a] he cannot enter the kingdom of God.);

The man of God (Romans 3: 15: And how can they preach unless they are sent? As it is written: How beautiful[a] are the feet of those[b] who announce the gospel of good things![)]); and *the Spirit of God* (John 3: 5; Titus 3: 5: He saved us— not by works of righteousness that we had done, but according to His mercy, through the washing of regeneration and renewal by the Holy Spirit).

FORGIVENESS

Not counting sins against us—remembering them no more forever (Ephesians 1: 7: We have redemption in Him through His blood, the forgiveness of our trespasses, according to the riches of His grace; Hebrews 10: 15-18: The Holy Spirit also testifies to us about this. For after He says: This is the covenant I will make with them after those days, says the Lord: I will put My laws on their hearts and write them on their minds, [17] He adds: I will never again remember their sins and their lawless acts. [18] Now where there is forgiveness of these, there is no longer an offering for sin.) I illustrate this with the woman taken in the act of adultery. Jesus forgave her (love) and told her to repent of her lifestyle (truth). In another place I point out how love and truth must be balanced, noting that truth without love is legalism, and love without truth is sentimentalism.

Forgetfulness and forgiveness are not the same thing. Some say, "If you haven't forgotten, you haven't forgiven." That is not true unless you mean by "forgetting" not remembering something against someone. Only God has a holy forgetfulness ("I will remember their sins no more." Sometimes when I pray Satan reminds me of my sins and I go again to God to ask forgiveness, and He replies, "I don't remember that sin—I have forgotten it—I remember planning to forget it.").

On the human level there are some things one can never forget. When my wife was 11-years-old she saw her mother shot to death. She can never forget that. However, she deliberately, through letter writing, led the woman responsible for her mother's death to the

Lord. My father went along with me to share the gospel with the drunk driver who killed my brother in an automobile accident. My wife and I still remember the burning pain over those losses, but we have totally forgiven those responsible for the burning pain. Therefore, I do not sympathize with someone who says they cannot forgive. Neither does God sympathize with them, for He has provided sufficient grace for them to forgive—grace based on His grace to forgive us all.

JUSTIFICATION

(Romans 5: 1: Therefore, since we have been declared righteous by faith, we have peace[a] with God through our Lord Jesus Christ.)

JUSTIFICATION
NEED: we have sinned against God
DEFINITION: Negative—not just to acquit, parole or pardon
Positive—No longer exposed to God's penalty
METHOD: faith and grace
RESULTS: our sins put on Christ's account Christ's righteousness put on our account

1) *The need for justification* (man has sinned against God (Romans 3: 3: What then? If some did not believe, will their unbelief cancel God's faithfulness?); **Jesus is the Judge** (John 5: 22: The Father, in fact, judges no one but has given all judgment to the Son,); **The jury is the Law of God and the deeds of man** (Romans 2: 6, He will repay each one according to his works: 12: All those who sinned without the law will also perish without the law, and all those who sinned under the law will be judged by the law); the verdict of "guilty" is returned (Romans 3: 9-20: What then? Are we any better?[a] Not at all! For we have previously charged that both Jews and Gentiles[b] are all under

sin,[°] [10] as it is written:[°]

There is no one righteous, not even one. [11] There is no one who understands; there is no one who seeks God.[12] All have turned away; all alike have become useless.

There is no one who does what is good, not even one.[°] [13] Their throat is an open grave; they deceive with their tongues.[f]Vipers' venom is under their lips.[g][14] Their mouth is full of cursing and bitterness.[h][15] Their feet are swift to shed blood;[16] ruin and wretchedness are in their paths,[17] and the path of peace they have not known.[][18] There is no fear of God before their eyes.[][19] Now we know that whatever the law says speaks to those who are subject to the law,[°] so that every mouth may be shut and the whole world may become subject to God's judgment.[] [20] For no one will be justified[m] in His sight by the works of the law, because the knowledge of sin comes through the law.);

the sentence is spiritual death (Romans 6: 23: For the wages of sin is death, but the gift of God is eternal life in Christ Jesus our Lord.)

2) *The definition of justification*   a. Negative: Not just acquitted (Romans 3: 19: Now we know that whatever the law says speaks to those who are subject to the law,[°] so that every mouth may be shut and the whole world may become subject to God's judgment); not just to be pardoned; not just to be paroled.

Positive: A. Strong: "By justification we mean that judicial act of God which, on account of Christ, to whom the sinner is united by faith, He declares that sinner to be no longer exposed to the penalty of the law but restored to His favor." It is the legal act whereby man's status before God is changed for the good.

3) *The method of justification* (Romans 4: 16: This is why the promise is by faith, so that it may be according to grace, to guarantee it to all the descendants—not only to those who are of the law[°] but also to those who are of Abraham's faith. He is the father of us all).

a. an act of faith (John 3: 14-16: Just as Moses lifted up the snake in the wilderness, so the Son of Man must be lifted up, [15] so that everyone who believes in Him will[a] have eternal life. [16] "For God loved the world in this way:[b] He gave His One and Only Son, so that everyone who believes in Him will not perish but have eternal life).

b. an act of grace (Ephesians 2: 1-10: And you were dead in your trespasses and sins [2] in which you previously walked according to the ways of this world, according to the ruler who exercises authority over the lower heavens,[a] the spirit now working in the disobedient.[b] [3] We too all previously lived among them in our fleshly desires, carrying out the inclinations of our flesh and thoughts, and we were by nature children under wrath as the others were also. [4] But God, who is rich in mercy, because of His great love that He had for us,[c] [5] made us alive with the Messiah even though we were dead in trespasses. You are saved by grace! [6] Together with Christ Jesus He also raised us up and seated us in the heavens, [7] so that in the coming ages He might display the immeasurable riches of His grace through His kindness to us in Christ Jesus. [8] For you are saved by grace through faith, and this is not from yourselves; it is God's gift— [9] not from works, so that no one can boast. [10] For we are His creation, created in Christ Jesus for good works).

4) *The results of justification*: Our sins imputed to Christ—the remission of sin's penalty (Romans 4: 7: [7] How joyful are those whose lawless acts are forgiven and whose sins are covered); Christ's righteousness is imputed to us (Romans 4: 11: And he received the sign of circumcision as a seal of the righteousness that he had by faith[a] while still uncircumcised. This was to make him the father of all who believe but are not circumcised, so that righteousness may be credited to them also.); and the restoration to divine favor (Romans 5: 1-11: Therefore, since we have been declared righteous by faith, we have peace[a] with God through our

Lord Jesus Christ. [2] We have also obtained access through Him by faith[b] into this grace in which we stand, and we rejoice in the hope of the glory of God. [3] And not only that, but we also rejoice in our afflictions, because we know that affliction produces endurance, [4] endurance produces proven character, and proven character produces hope. [5] This hope will not disappoint us, because God's love has been poured out in our hearts through the Holy Spirit who was given to us.

Those Declared Righteous Are Reconciled

[6] For while we were still helpless, at the appointed moment, Christ died for the ungodly. [7] For rarely will someone die for a just person—though for a good person perhaps someone might even dare to die. [8] But God proves His own love for us in that while we were still sinners, Christ died for us! [9] Much more then, since we have now been declared righteous by His blood, we will be saved through Him from wrath. [10] For if, while we were enemies, we were reconciled to God through the death of His Son, then how much more, having been reconciled, will we be saved by His life! [11] And not only that, but we also rejoice in God through our Lord Jesus Christ. We have now received this reconciliation through Him.).

I have a bank account that guarantees payment of a check I write when I knowingly or unknowingly don't have sufficient funds to pay the check. The bank automatically imputes funds to my account, so the check may be honored—the only caveat being that I have to pay back the funds imputed. God imputes the righteousness of Jesus Christ to our spiritual accounts the same as He imputed our sins to Jesus' account at the Cross. The major difference is that God's imputation of Jesus' righteousness to our spiritual accounts is that we don't have to pay it back—we can't pay it back—it is the free gift of God through His grace.

SANCTIFICATION

SANCTIFICATION

Not eradication of sinful nature.

Not a "second blessing"

To "Set Apart"

H.L. Wilmington on Romans 6:

What we can know (1-10)

What we can account (11-12)

How we can yield (16-23)

How we can obey (16, 21-22)

(John 17: 19: [19] I sanctify Myself for them, so they also may be sanctified by the truth; 1 Thessalonians 4: 3: For this is God's will, your sanctification: that you abstain from sexual immorality; 1 Thessalonians 5: 23: Now may the God of peace Himself sanctify you completely. And may your spirit, soul, and body be kept sound and blameless for the coming of our Lord Jesus Christ.).

1) *Definition of sanctification*: It is not the eradication of the sinful nature (Philippians 3: 12-14: Not that I have already reached the goal or am already fully mature, but I make every effort to take hold of it because I also have been taken hold of by Christ Jesus. [13] Brothers, I do not[a] consider myself to have taken hold of it. But one thing I do: Forgetting what is behind and reaching forward to what is ahead, [14] I pursue as my goal the prize promised by God's heavenly[b] call in Christ Jesus.); Not a "second blessing" Note: many take 2 Corinthians 1: 15 (I planned with this confidence to come to you first, so you could have a double benefit) where Paul talks about a "second benefit" to mean a "second blessing", but Paul has already spoken of them as being sanctified (1 Corinthians 1: 2: To God's church at Corinth, to those who are

sanctified in Christ Jesus and called as saints, with all those in every place who call on the name of Jesus Christ our Lord—both their Lord and ours.; 6: 11: And some of you used to be like this. But you were washed, you were sanctified, you were justified in the name of the Lord Jesus Christ and by the Spirit of our God);

Not the baptism of the Holy Spirit—all believers are baptized in the Holy Spirit regardless of spiritual condition (1 Corinthians 3: 1-4: Brothers, I was not able to speak to you as spiritual people but as people of the flesh, as babies in Christ. 2 I gave you milk to drink, not solid food, because you were not yet ready for it. In fact, you are still not ready, 3 because you are still fleshly. For since there is envy and strife[a] among you, are you not fleshly and living like unbelievers?[b] 4 For whenever someone says, "I'm with Paul," and another, "I'm with Apollos," are you not unspiritual people?[ɔ]).

The basic meaning is "to set apart". In the Bible vessels were set apart for holy use, days and seasons were set apart, people can be set apart for different reasons.

Wilmington has a contrast that is helpful:

> Justification deals with our standing; sanctification deals with our state.
>
> Justification is that which God does **for** us, while sanctification is that which God does **in** us (bold emphasis mine).
>
> Justification is an act, while sanctification is a work or process.
>
> Justification is the means, while sanctification is the end.
>
> Justification makes us safe, while sanctification makes us sound.
>
> Justification declares us good, while sanctification makes us good.

Justification removes the guilt and penalty of sin, while sanctification checks the growth and power of sin.

Justification furnishes the track which leads to heaven, while sanctification furnishes the train.

2) Romans 6 shows us 4 commands that help us understand sanctification. According to H. L. Wilmington, there are four things we can experience as a result of God's sanctification in us. These four things are found in Romans, chapter 6.

a. What we can <u>know</u> Romans 6: 1-10: What should we say then? Should we continue in sin so that grace may multiply? [2] Absolutely not! How can we who died to sin still live in it? [3] Or are you unaware that all of us who were baptized into Christ Jesus were baptized into His death? [4] Therefore we were buried with Him by baptism into death, in order that, just as Christ was raised from the dead by the glory of the Father, so we too may walk in a new way[a] of life. [5] For if we have been joined with Him in the likeness of His death, we will certainly also be[b] in the likeness of His resurrection. [6] For we know that our old self[c] was crucified with Him in order that sin's dominion over the body[d] may be abolished, so that we may no longer be enslaved to sin, [7] since a person who has died is freed[e] from sin's claims.[f] [8] Now if we died with Christ, we believe that we will also live with Him, [9] because we know that Christ, having been raised from the dead, will not die again. Death no longer rules over Him. [10] For in light of the fact that He died, He died to sin once for all; but in light of the fact that He lives, He lives to God.):

b. What we can <u>reckon or account</u>—"reckon" means we are to act upon the aforementioned facts regardless of any personal feelings (Romans 6: 11-12: So, you too consider yourselves dead to sin but alive to God in Christ Jesus.[a][12] Therefore do not let sin reign in your mortal body, so that you obey[b] its desires.).

c. What we can yield to the Holy Spirit (Romans 6: 16-23: Don't you know that if you offer yourselves to someone[a] as obedient slaves, you are slaves of that one you obey—either of sin leading to death or of obedience leading to righteousness? [17] But thank God that, although you used to be slaves of sin, you obeyed from the heart that pattern of teaching you were transferred[b] to, [18] and having been liberated from sin, you became enslaved to righteousness. [19] I am using a human analogy[c] because of the weakness of your flesh.[d] For just as you offered the parts[e] of yourselves as slaves to moral impurity, and to greater and greater lawlessness, so now offer them as slaves to righteousness, which results in sanctification. [20] For when you were slaves of sin, you were free from allegiance to righteousness.[f] [21] So what fruit was produced[g] then from the things you are now ashamed of? For the end of those things is death. [22] But now, since you have been liberated from sin and have become enslaved to God, you have your fruit, which results in sanctification[h]—and the end is eternal life! [23] For the wages of sin is death, but the gift of God is eternal life in Christ Jesus our Lord.). Stop yielding to unrighteousness as a practice and start yielding to righteousness as a once for all act.

d. What we can obey (Romans 6: 16, 21-22: So what fruit was produced[a] then from the things you are now ashamed of? For the end of those things is death. [22] But now, since you have been liberated from sin and have become enslaved to God, you have your fruit, which results in sanctification[b]—and the end is eternal life!). Obey a new Master; obey a new doctrine; because we are freed from sin, and we are to desire the fruits of the Spirit.

Glorification:

GLORIFICATION MEANING:

Absolute perfection for all believers

PURPOSE: completes justification and sanctification

TIME: beginning at the Rapture and continuing for eternity

RESULTS: a body like Christ's resurrected body
A body of flesh and bones
A recognizable body
A Holy Spirit dominated body
An eternal body

This speaks of the completeness of salvation (1 Thessalonians 5: 23, 24: Now may the God of peace Himself sanctify you completely. And may your spirit, soul, and body be kept sound and blameless for the coming of our Lord Jesus Christ. [24] He who calls you is faithful, who also will do it.; Jude 1: 24-25: Now to Him who is able to protect you from stumbling and to make you stand in the presence of His glory, blameless and with great joy, [25] to the only God our Savior, through Jesus Christ our Lord,[a] be glory, majesty, power, and authority before all time,[b] now and forever. Amen).Note: when Adam and Eve sinned in the Garden of Eden, they died in three ways—immediately in their spirits, progressively in their souls, and ultimately in their bodies. Likewise, when we are saved, we come alive in the same three ways—immediately in our spirits, progressively in our souls, and ultimately in our bodies.

1) <u>The body is saved</u> (1 Corinthians 15: 44: [44] sown a natural body, raised a spiritual body. If there is a natural

body, there is also a spiritual body; Philippians 3: 2: He will transform the body of our humble condition into the likeness of His glorious body, by the power that enables Him to subject everything to Himself1; Romans 8: 23: And not only that, but we ourselves who have the Spirit as the firstfruits—we also groan within ourselves, eagerly waiting for adoption, the redemption of our bodies.).

Body saved

Soul saved·

Spirit saved

2) The soul is saved (Hebrews 6: 19: We have this hope as an anchor for our lives, safe and secure. It enters the inner sanctuary behind the curtain; James 1; 21: Therefore, ridding yourselves of all moral filth and evil,[a] humbly receive the implanted word, which is able to save you; 1 Peter 4: 19: So those who suffer according to God's will should, while doing what is good, entrust themselves to a faithful Creator).

3) The spirit is saved (Romans 8: 16: The Spirit Himself testifies together with our spirit that we are God's children; 2 Timothy 4: 22: The Lord be with your spirit. Grace be with you; Hebrews 12: 23: to the assembly of the firstborn whose names have been written[a] in heaven, to God who is the Judge of all, to the spirits of righteous people made perfect).

GLORIFICATION: (Romans 8: 30: And those He predestined, He also called; and those He called, He also justified; and those He justified, He also glorified.; Romans 8: 18: For I consider that the sufferings of this present time are not worth comparing with the glory that is going to be revealed to us.; Colossians 3: 4: When the Messiah, who is your[a] life, is revealed, then you also will be revealed with Him in glory; I John 3: 1-3: Look at how great a love[a] the Father has given us that we should be called God's children. And we are! The reason the world does not know us is that it didn't know Him. 2 Dear friends, we are God's children now, and what we will be has not yet been revealed. We know that when He appears, we will be like Him because we will see Him as He is. 3 And everyone who has this hope in Him purifies himself just as He is pure).

1) The meaning of glorification: it refers to the ultimate and absolute physical, mental, and spiritual perfections of all believers (Romans 8: 22, 23: For we know that the whole creation has been groaning together with labor pains until now. [23] And not only that, but we ourselves who have the Spirit as the firstfruits—we also groan within ourselves, eagerly waiting for adoption, the redemption of our bodies.).

2) The purpose of glorification: it completes justification and sanctification—in the past, Christ the Prophet saved us from the penalty of sin through justification; in the present, Christ the Priest saves us from the power of sin through sanctification; and, in the future, Christ the King shall save us from the presence of sin through glorification.

3) The time of glorification—beginning at the Rapture of the Church and continuing throughout eternity (1 Thessalonians 4: 13-18: We do not want you to be uninformed, brothers, concerning those who are asleep, so that you will not grieve like the rest, who have no hope. [14] Since we believe that Jesus died and rose again, in the same way God will bring with Him those who have fallen asleep through[a] Jesus. [15] For we say this to you by a revelation from the Lord:[b] We who are still alive at the Lord's coming will certainly have no advantage over[c] those who have fallen asleep. [16] For the Lord Himself will descend from heaven with a shout,[d] with the archangel's voice, and with the trumpet of God, and the dead in Christ will rise first. [17] Then we who are still alive will be caught up together with them in the clouds to meet the Lord in the air and so we will always be with the Lord. [18] Therefore encourage[e] one another with these words).

4) The results of glorification—what kind of body will we have?

a. *Like Christ's resurrected body* (Philippians 3: 21: He will transform the body of our humble condition into the likeness of His glorious body, by the power that enables Him to subject everything to Himself)

b. *Body of flesh and bones* (Luke 24: 39: Look at My hands and My feet, that it is I Myself! Touch Me and see, because a ghost does not have flesh and bones as you can see, I have)

c. *A recognizable body* (1 Corinthians 13: 12: [12] For now we see indistinctly,[a] as in a mirror,[b] but then face to face. Now I know in part, but then I will know fully, as I am fully known).

d. *A body in which the Holy Spirit dominates* (1 Corinthians 15: 44: sown a natural body, raised a spiritual body. If there is a natural body, there is also a spiritual body, 49: [49] And just as we have borne the image of the man made of dust, we will also bear the image of the heavenly man).

e. *A body unlimited by time or space* (John 20: 19: In the evening of that first day of the week, the disciples were gathered together with the doors locked because of their fear of the Jews. Then Jesus came, stood among them, and said to them, "Peace to you!", 26: After eight days His disciples were indoors again, and Thomas was with them. Even though the doors were locked, Jesus came and stood among them. He said, "Peace to you!").

f. *An eternal body* (2 Corinthians 5: 2: Indeed, we groan in this body, desiring to put on our dwelling from heaven).

g. *A glorious body* (1 Corinthians 15: 43: [43] sown in dishonor, raised in glory; sown in weakness, raised in power.

5. Two fundamental ideas in soteriology from Louis Sperry Chafer:

   a. To be saved is to be rescued from a lost estate.

   b. To be saved is to be brought into a saved estate.

c. We can either warn people to flee from wrath or to woo them to God's love.

d. Lost people are under Satan's rule and need to be rescued (Colossians 1: 13: He has rescued us from the domain of darkness and transferred us into the kingdom of the Son He loves).

e. Mankind is born in a fallen state, condemned by inherited sin nature and because of his personal sins, and needs to be born again.

f. Salvation provides a dismissal and removal of every charge against mankind.

WHY STUDY SOTERIOLOGY?

(According to Louis Sperry Chafer)

1. God's message includes the whole human family in its outreach, and since the great proportion are unregenerate, and since the gospel of salvation is the only word addressed to the unsaved, it is reasonable to conclude that, in a well-balanced ministry, gospel preaching should account for no less than seventy-five percent of the pulpit testimony.

a. The rest may be for the edification of the believers.

b. Since seventy-five percent of our preaching should be to the lost, it remains a safe conclusion that we need to know soteriology completely.

2. The preacher is an important link in the chain leading sinners to the cross the other links are:

a. There is no deficiency in Christ's atonement

b. There is no flaw in God's Word

c. There is no weakness with the Holy Spirit

d. There should be no omissions or defects in gospel preaching.

e. There should be an increase in dependence upon God for all gospel preaching (Galatians 1: 8-9: But even if we or an angel from heaven should preach to you a gospel other than what we have preached to you, a curse be on him![a] 9 As we have said before, I now say again: If anyone preaches to you a gospel contrary to what you received, a curse be on him). This anathema has never been revoked.

f. From the human point of view the preacher may misguide someone as to the way of salvation, and thereby condemn the soul of the hearer.

g. From the heavenly point of view, God has given His Son to redeem us; how dare we not present Him as the only way of salvation?

h. This emphasizes 2 Timothy 2: 15: Be diligent to present yourself approved to God, a worker who doesn't need to be ashamed, correctly teaching the word of truth.

SOTERIOLOGY IS THE TOTAL PACKAGE FROM THE TOTAL TRINITY (Based on the writings of Louis Sperry Chafer)

1. The Christian was saved in the past when he believed (Acts 16: 30-31: Then he escorted them out and said, "Sirs, what must I do to be saved?"31 So they said, "Believe on the Lord Jesus, and you will be saved—you and your household." ; Ephesians 2: 8: For you are saved by grace through faith, and this is not from yourselves; it is God's gift).

a. Saved from sin's penalty or damnation.

b. At the moment of salvation saved eternally from a lost estate.

2. The believer is being saved in the present (Romans 6: 1-14: What should we say then? Should we continue in sin so that grace may

multiply? [2] Absolutely not! How can we who died to sin still live in it? [3] Or are you unaware that all of us who were baptized into Christ Jesus were baptized into His death? [4] Therefore we were buried with Him by baptism into death, in order that, just as Christ was raised from the dead by the glory of the Father, so we too may walk in a new way[a] of life. [5] For if we have been joined with Him in the likeness of His death, we will certainly also be[b] in the likeness of His resurrection. [6] For we know that our old self[c] was crucified with Him in order that sin's dominion over the body[d] may be abolished, so that we may no longer be enslaved to sin, [7] since a person who has died is freed[e] from sin's claims.[f]

[8] Now if we died with Christ, we believe that we will also live with Him, [9] because we know that Christ, having been raised from the dead, will not die again. Death no longer rules over Him. [10] For in light of the fact that He died, He died to sin once for all; but in light of the fact that He lives, He lives to God. [11] So, you too consider yourselves dead to sin but alive to God in Christ Jesus.[g][12] Therefore do not let sin reign in your mortal body, so that you obey[h] its desires. [13] And do not offer any parts[i] of it to sin as weapons for unrighteousness. But as those who are alive from the dead, offer yourselves to God, and all the parts[j] of yourselves to God as weapons for righteousness. [14] For sin will not rule over you, because you are not under law but under grace).

    a. Saved from sin's power or dominion.

    b. Divinely preserved and sanctified.

3. The Christian shall be saved from sin's presence or devastation (1 Peter 1: 3-5: Praise the God and Father of our Lord Jesus Christ. According to His great mercy, He has given us a new birth into a living hope through the resurrection of Jesus Christ from the dead [4] and into an inheritance that is imperishable, uncorrupted, and unfading, kept in heaven for you. [5] You are being protected by God's power through faith for a salvation that is ready to be revealed in the last time).

    a. Faultless in glory.

b. Forever with the Lord.

SALVATION IS FROM JEHOVAH

(Jonah 2: 9: [9] but as for me, I will sacrifice to You with a voice of thanksgiving.

I will fulfill what I have vowed.

Salvation[a] is from the LORD; Psalm 3: 8:

Salvation belongs to the LORD; may Your blessing be on Your people. *Selah*).

1. **Sustained by both revelation and by reason**.

   a. From revelation—the Scriptures speak over and over of such.

   b. From reason—faith is the vehicle by which salvation comes—two angles.

   1) From the legal aspect—God is just and must be consistent with Himself—He had to devise a means of propitiation and grace.

   2) From the practical aspect—man cannot forgive himself, cannot save himself, and is thrown upon the mercy of God.

2. **Jesus Christ is the Source of salvation**.

   a. He is able to save—our "kinsman redeemer". (Hebrews 2: 18: For since He Himself was tested and has suffered, He is able to help those who are tested Ephesians 3: 20: Now to Him who is able to do above and beyond all that we ask or think according to the power that works in us)

   b. He is willing to save (Matthew 8: 2-3: Right away a man with a serious skin   disease came up and knelt before Him, saying, "Lord, if You are willing, You can make me clean." [3] Reaching out His hand He touched him, saying, "I am willing; be made clean." Immediately his disease was healed. [; 2 Peter 3: 9: The Lord does not delay His promise, as some understand delay, but is patient with you, not wanting any to perish but all to come to repentance).

THE DIVINE MOTIVES IN SALVATION (Gathered from Louis Sperry Chafer and E. Y. Mullins)

1. Salvation is more important to God than to us, because of HIS INFINITE LOVE. If He could not save, He could not express His love (John 3: 16: For God loved the world in this way:[a] He gave His One and Only Son, so that everyone who believes in Him will not perish but have eternal life.).

GOD'S MOTIVES IN SALVATION

His love could not be expressed without it.

We are saved to do good works

We don't perish, but have eternal life

God's grace needs room to bloom

So, Jesus didn't die for nothing

That God may redeem

2.. He saves us to do good works (Ephesians 2: 8-10: For you are saved by grace through faith, and this is not from yourselves; it is God's gift— 9 not from works, so that no one can boast. 10 For we are His creation, created in Christ Jesus for good works, which God prepared ahead of time so that we should walk in them)—we are not saved by works, but to do good works.

3. The advantages that come to us by being saved—do not perish; do receive everlasting life.

4. That God's grace may have an adequate manifestation. (Ephesians 2: 7: so that in the coming ages He might display the immeasurable riches of His grace through His kindness to us in Christ Jesus.). This is a part of God that angels had not seen—

God's divine grace upon undeserving sinners.

5. <u>That Jesus' death may not be in vain</u>. This is beyond our ability to understand (Romans 8: 29: For those He foreknew He also predestined to be conformed to the image of His Son, so that He would be the firstborn among many brothers; 1 John 3: 1-2: Look at how great a love[a] the Father has given us that we should be called God's children. And we are! The reason the world does not know us is that it didn't know Him. [2] Dear friends, we are God's children now, and what we will be has not yet been revealed. We know that when He appears, we will be like Him because we will see Him as He is; 1 Corinthians 15: 49: And just as we have borne the image of the man made of dust, we will also bear the image of the heavenly man; Colossians 1: 27: God wanted to make known among the Gentiles the glorious wealth of this mystery, which is Christ in you, the hope of glory; Philippians 3: 21: He will transform the body of our humble condition into the likeness of His glorious body, by the power that enables Him to subject everything to Himself).

6.. <u>That He may redeem His creation</u> (the universe): Romans 8: 18-25: For I consider that the sufferings of this present time are not worth comparing with the glory that is going to be revealed to us. [19] For the creation eagerly awaits with anticipation for God's sons to be revealed. [20] For the creation was subjected to futility—not willingly, but because of Him who subjected it—in the hope [21] that the creation itself will also be set free from the bondage of corruption into the glorious freedom of God's children. [22] For we know that the whole creation has been groaning together with labor pains until now. [23] And not only that, but we ourselves who have the Spirit as the firstfruits—we also groan within ourselves, eagerly waiting for adoption, the redemption of our bodies. [24] Now in this hope we were saved, yet hope that is seen is not hope, because who hopes for what he sees? [25] But if we hope for what we do not see, we eagerly wait for it with patience

DIVINE PERFECTIONS (The salvation God gives is perfect—from the writings of Chafer). We see this from the following arguments:

1. That by the death of Christ, all judgment and condemnation are so perfectly borne that they can never again be reckoned against the believer (Romans 8: 1: Therefore, no condemnation now exists for those in Christ Jesus).

2. That by the resurrection of Christ, every requirement for eternal association with God in heaven is bestowed—all, indeed, on the principle of uncomplicated grace

3. That salvation may be secure (Colossians 3: 3: [3] For you have died, and your life is hidden with the Messiah in God)

a. Many Scriptures seem to indicate that one can lose his salvation, but when they are viewed in context, there is a logical explanation. Some of these passages deal with false teachers, some with conversion without repentance, some with Christian rewards, some with missing God's best, some with God's discipline, some with fruit-bearing, some with false doctrines, some with the sin unto death, some with the unpardonable sin, some with Gentile nations, and some with local churches.

b. There is the possibility of apostasy, but an apostate was not saved (See the parable of the Sower—the hard ground (non-conversion), the shallow ground (emotional conversion), and the thorny ground (intellectual conversion), were never saved—they produced no fruit.

c. Reasoned from the work of the Father, the Son and the Holy Spirit.

1) The work of the Father (His plan to save and His power to save: Romans 8: 30: And those He predestined, He also

called; and those He called, He also justified; and those He justified, He also glorified.

2) The work of the Son (His work on the cross, His promises, His prayer: John 5: 24: I assure you: Anyone who hears My word and believes Him who sent Me has eternal life and will not come under judgment but has passed from death to life; 6: 37: Everyone the Father gives Me will come to Me, and the one who comes to Me I will never cast out; 10: 27-29: My sheep hear My voice, I know them, and they follow Me. [28] I give them eternal life, and they will never perish—ever! No one will snatch them out of My hand. [29] My Father, who has given them to Me, is greater than all. No one is able to snatch them out of the Father's hand.

3) The work of the Holy Spirit (His regeneration, His baptism, His indwelling, His seal: John 3: 3-7: Jesus replied, "I assure you: Unless someone is born again,[a] he cannot see the kingdom of God."

[4] "But how can anyone be born when he is old?" Nicodemus asked Him. "Can he enter his mother's womb a second time and be born?"

[5] Jesus answered, "I assure you: Unless someone is born of water and the Spirit,[b] he cannot enter the kingdom of God. [6] Whatever is born of the flesh is flesh, and whatever is born of the Spirit is spirit. [7] Do not be amazed that I told you that you[c] must be born again. ; Romans 6: 3: Or are you unaware that all of us who were baptized into Christ Jesus were baptized into His death?; John 7: 37-39: On the last and most important day of the festival, Jesus stood up and cried out, "If anyone is thirsty, he should come to Me[a] and drink! [38] The one who believes in Me, as the Scripture has said,[b] will have streams of living water flow from deep within him." [39] He said this about the Spirit. Those who believed in Jesus were going to receive the Spirit, for the Spirit[c] had not

yet been received[d][e] because Jesus had not yet been glorified; Ephesians 1: 13: When you heard the message of truth, the gospel of your salvation, and when you believed in Him, you were also sealed with the promised Holy Spirit).

4) Consider the purposes of John in his gospel and his first epistle: John 20:31: But these are written so that you may believe Jesus is the Messiah, the Son of God,[a] and by believing you may have life in His name; 1 John 5: 13: I have written these things to you who believe in the name of the Son of God, so that you may know that you have eternal life.

There is a story of an old preacher whose church sent off one of their brightest young men to university. There came a time when the young man returned and announced he no longer believed in eternal security, and that he would like to debate the old pastor on the subject. The old pastor accepted his challenge. The date was set and publicized. On the night of the debate the church building was overflowing.

The young man with his mental acuity and theological training made a powerful argument, and had the audience swayed to his side. Then came the old pastor's turn. He announced he would not take long and that he had asked the deacons to assist him. They brought in three wooden barrels—one 5 gallons, one 10 gallons, and one 20 gallons. The old pastor read Colossians 3: 3: "You have died, and your life is hidden in Christ with God." He announced that the 5-gallon barrel represented the believer, that the 10-gallon barrel represented Jesus Christ, and that the 20 gallon barrel represented God the Father

He then asked the deacons to take the 5-gallon barrel (the believer) and place it in the 10-gallon barrel (Jesus Christ). He then had them nail on the lid. Next, he had them place both barrels into the 20-gallon barrel (God the Father). They did so, nailing the lid on that one as well.

The old pastor then made a challenge: I dare any person in this place to get at the 5-gallon barrel (the believer) without having to go through the 10 gallon barrel (Jesus Christ) and the 20-gallon barrel (God the Father), repeating, "You have died and your life is hidden in Christ with God." The debate was over. It was obvious who won. Not the old pastor, but every believer. No one can pluck them from My hand. My Father who is greater than all will not let anyone pluck the believer from His hand (a paraphrase from John 10).

Note: I have chosen not to address election, because I will not try to teach that which I do not understand. Three statements will suffice: 1) If God didn't elect some, none would come; 2) We can trust what we don't understand. I don't understand how a large jet can be airborne—oh! I know what aerodynamics teaches, but I don't understand it—yet, I use air travel very frequently to get me to the mission field: I don't understand how Television works—the sound and sight waves in the air being able to be heard and seen because I have the right receiver—yet, I enjoy watching my favorite sports teams play, even if they are thousands of miles away. Incidentally, here is an illustration of our relationship with God in that we are the receivers through which the lost world sees God. As Jesus was the revelation of God, so we are the mini-un-coverings of what God is like; and 3) The counsel of His will is beyond human understanding and I take solace in Psalm 131: 1-3:

Colossians 3: 3, and a debate about eternal security

[1] LORD, my heart is not proud; my eyes are not haughty. I do not get involved with things too great or too difficult for me.

[2] Instead, I have calmed and quieted myself like a little weaned child with its mother; I am like a little child. [3] Israel, put your hope in the LORD, both now and forever).

THE CROSS: NOT JUST FOR US, BUT ALSO BY US

In the message of evangelism, we should point out that the cross is not just something done **for us**. It is also something done **by us**. Jesus went to the cross to pay for the crimes that I have committed.

Once, I had a man join me on the golf course. When he gave me his name, I did not notice anything unusual about it. As we played around the course, I was sharing with him the facts of the gospel. As we approached the 16th box, he asked me, "Wayne, who was responsible for the death of Jesus?" Then his name became significant. He was a Jew and wanted to know if I blamed him and other Jews for Jesus' death. I whispered a prayer, "Help me Holy Spirit."

Here is the answer God gave me. "Mr. _____, physically, the Romans killed Jesus; politically, the Jews killed Him. But spiritually, you and I killed Him. It was for our sins that He died."

Within a few moments I was able to pray with him. I can only trust God with the decision he made. I can also know that I presented the two rails of the antinomy to him: Jesus was ordained by God to die for the sins of the whole wide world, yet, each of us bears responsibility for His death.

Thank God that He didn't stay dead but arose to life. Therefore, He can give us abundant life in this present age, and eternal life here on earth an in heaven with Him. Our job is to prepare people to inhabit the mansion He built for them. That is evangelism, the message of evangelism, and joy of obedience wrapped into one package.

It is so simple it is almost simplistic. The language is simple. The **language** of the New Testament is the language of the common person. If we wish to evangelize, we must speak the language that the lost person understands.

The **story** is simple. It is the story of One who died, was buried and rose again. At Pentecost Peter took advantage of the event, took a text from Joel, and preached Jesus, and 3,000 people were saved. What a pattern for preaching! (1) Take advantage of an event, (2) take a biblical text and (3) watch God save people. There was a very intelligent man who was trying to find Christ. He even went to prayer meetings and took his Bible. His pastor talked to him many times and yet he was not saved. Finally, one day his 10-year-old daughter came in and said, "Daddy, today I asked Jesus to come into my heart and He did." There it was. That man simply prayed and asked Christ to come into his heart and was saved. The simple story as a child who told that the One who died for her had come into her heart led him to Christ.

Six Kinds of Evangelism

by Leighton Ford

Mass evangelism

Personal evangelism

Impromptu evangelism

Dialogue evangelism

Systematic evangelism

Literary evangelism

THE METHOD OF EVANGELISM (SYSTEM)

The method is very modern and very relevant. **The method is incarnation**. "He became flesh and dwelt among us." He identified with the people and taught them the way of life. He said, "As My Father has sent me, so I send you (As I have identified with the people, so I send you to identify with them that they may have life). You have to get inside the other person's skin as Ezekiel said, "I sat where they sat."

Two truths in the Bible create trouble for us. The words of Paul to come out from among them and be separate, and the words of Jesus to go into all the world and make disciples. We have trouble balancing the coming out and the going out. Some have come out and have enjoyed the church and made a club of it. There is a delicate balance, but you never have evangelism in isolation; you have evangelism only in involvement. It is time we realize that the church is more than a place where we organize our bowling and ball teams. It is a lighthouse in the darkness of sin to show people the way to God.

> ### METHOD OF EVANGELISM
>
> *Incarnation*
>
> *Preaching*
>
> *Holy Spirit control*

The method is also by preaching but preaching alone will not get the job done. Paul said, "I have become all things to all people that I may save (gain) some."

SIX METHODS OF EVANGELISM

The New Testament is creative in its methods. Leighton Ford in his book, *"The Christian Persuader,* lists six different methods of evangelism. Here are the methods along with my comments.

1. **Mass evangelism** *as seen in the work of Jesus, Peter and Paul.* Actually, there is really no such thing as mass evangelism. There is mass communication of the gospel—public evangelism. I repeat myself: Dogs and cats are born in litters, but people are brought into the kingdom of God one-by-one. It was my privilege to preach many interdenominational crusades and see thousands of people come to the Lord in those dynamic settings. It is much easier to get lost people to attend a service in a neutral setting than to get them into a church building. This is still a valid method.

2. **Personal evangelism** *as seen in the 25 interviews of Jesus with individuals.* I made a practice of visiting enough each week that I had at least one person committed to walk the aisle on Sunday. Dr. Jeff Iorg, President of Gateway Seminary, said he did a similar thing—visiting sufficiently that he had reasonable expectation of someone coming forward. I had my team in Pusan, South Korea. We had finished our scheduled meetings and were awaiting our departure back to Seoul. It was drizzling rain. We had our copies of my gospel tract (normally printed in red, but in South Korea they were in green because of the implications of red communism). I walked out into the rain and approached the truck driver who was to deliver our luggage to the train station. I had no interpreter and he knew no English. I placed one of the tracts into his hand, placed my hands together in a manner of prayer, pointed to heaven and then to his heart. I took my finger and ran over the tract, sentence by sentence. When I got to the prayer, I again pointed to heaven, to his heart, placed my hands together and began to pray. In a moment I felt him tap me on the shoulder. I looked up. His eyes were full of

tears, but he was smiling. He pointed to heaven, placed his hands together in a prayer style, pointed to his heart. I knew for sure that he had accepted Jesus as Lord and Savior of his life.

3. **Impromptu evangelism** as seen at the Gate Beautiful or the woman at the well. I have been privileged to win many people in market places, on planes, at ball games, while out shopping, at restaurants, etc. I was in a southern city of Ethiopia ministering. I became ill from exhaustion and had to miss a man-made appointment. I stayed in my room and rested until the fever was gone. I complained to God about getting sick and missing my man-made appointment. However, God had an appointment for me (a God-made appointment).

I went into the lobby since the internet would not work in my room. There were four of the hotel maids sitting and working. Since the major motels require that their employees be able to speak English, they could perfectly understand me. The Holy Spirit whispered in my spirit: *this is why you were sick; you are not to go on the internet; you are to witness to these ladies.*

I began to share the gospel with them. They listened attentively, and about 20 minutes later they all prayed to receive Christ as Lord and Savior. This was the result of the Holy Spirit giving me an impromptu opportunity to do evangelism.

I "face-timed" my wife, Gloria, at 3: 00 a.m. (her time) to introduce these ladies to her. Of course, she had to arrange her hair (lol). As I introduced them to her, she spoke a word of encouragement to them and we hung up.

After I hung up from "face-time", I told these ladies that I had done that for two reasons: one, I wanted them to meet my wife; and, two, I pointed out that since they could talk to my wife more than 10,000 miles away, they should never doubt that God could hear them whenever they prayed.

On a mission trip to Nevada I had another impromptu experience of sharing the gospel. The pastor and I took some new believers out to a developed natural hot spring to baptize them. When we arrived, there were around 15-18 people soaking in the spa. I asked them if they would mind being interrupted long enough for us to baptize these people. They politely agreed. When the pastor got the first new believer into the water I asked if I could explain what was happening. They again agreed. For about 12 minutes I explained the gospel. They watched intently as the pastor baptized the new believers. When he had finished baptizing the ones we brought, I asked, "Are there any of you ready to openly confess Christ as your Lord and Savior by letting the pastor baptize you?" It was amazing how many of them came forward and let the pastor baptize them. I have also used this technique when I have baptized at the beaches of Southern California.

4. **Dialogue evangelism** *as seen in Paul on Mars Hill*. Be friendly, starting conversations and let the Holy Spirit lead the thoughts where He pleases. Ask questions like, "Who is the most important person you have ever met?" Then share that Jesus is the most important person you ever met and lead them to the point that they know how to receive Him. Once my wife and I were camping and I was not ready to go to bed, though I needed to turn off the lights, so my wife and children could get some sleep. So, I left the camping trailer and went over to the bar. There were about a dozen people in the bar. I ordered myself a soda, pulled up a bar stool in the middle of the room, and said, "Folks, I am happy to be here among you. I don't habitually go to bars, because I don't drink alcoholic beverages. However, I have come to share with you Someone who can take the place of the high you get from alcohol."

I dialogued with them for about 25 minutes about the gospel of Jesus Christ. I offered them an opportunity to pray and receive Christ as Lord and Savior. Four of them responded positively and prayed aloud in front of their comrades to accept Jesus.

5. **Systematic evangelism** *as seen in the sending of the seventy, two-by-two, or in Acts 5: 42.* I preached that people should

evangelize, but no one was evangelizing. I prayed. God showed me what to do. I asked my wife to get a baby sitter and accompany me on personal visitation. I instructed her to watch carefully what I did. After leading several people to Christ in several homes, I knocked on the door of the next house, and told her, "This one is yours." She was alarmed but couldn't back out. She fumbled all over the gospel, but two boys were saved. When we went to the next house, she said, "This one is mine also." Evangelism is more caught than taught.

6. *Literary evangelism as seen in the gospels of Luke and John.* My wife wrote her step-mother-in-law and led her to Christ through her letter. With the new means of communication (texting, face-book, etc.) there are many opportunities for evangelism with the literary method.

Involved with our methods are three physical motions: (1) get up, (2) turn the knob on the TV to OFF, and (3) use the Nike slogan: "JUST DO IT."

As Christians, we need to be at it. It is much better to have tried and failed than not to have tried at all, but when we try to witness in Christ's name we cannot fail. Faithfulness is success.

Our greatest method is found in being empowered or rather OVER-POWERED by the Holy Spirit. The Holy Spirit calls and gathers and sanctifies and sends us into the world to glorify Christ by edifying His church through evangelism. The same Spirit who led us to Christ in the beginning gives us strength for the redemptive task. He comes alongside us to help us when we try to witness. We have a formidable foe (Satan), but we have a greater One alongside us. We have power to stand up to our foe. We need not be afraid to tell the story. He will help us.

There are four simple things that have always worked and will always work. Sin is the same in Seattle as in Miami, and the grace of God is the same in Boston as San Diego. The four main things worked in Paul's day will work in our day. Paul used them in the presence of Agrippa (Acts 26). Here are the four things:

1. **Use the Scriptures**. Nothing can take the place of Scripture. The Psalmist did not say, "Thy Word have I hidden in my POCKET that I may not sin against you." He said, "Thy Word have I hidden in my HEART that I may not sin against you." We need to commit Scripture to memory. One may well compare the amount of time he spends watching TV and reading the internet to the amount of time he spends studying (not just reading) his Bible. Also, always validate your message and ministry by using the Bible as your authentication. Don't argue to prove the Bible—it can take care of itself. Just share the Bible with those who will listen.

2. **Give the simple facts of the gospel**. Don't try to give meat to a baby, nor to a lost person. He cannot understand it (1 Corinthians 2: 14). Here are the simple facts of the gospel (Scripture references are not given since they are so numerous):

    a. Man was made to belong to God, but sin has separated him from God.

    b. Christ Jesus came to die for man's sinful rebellion. God became flesh and bore man's sin.

    c. In His death and burial Christ suffered man's hell.

    d. In His resurrection Christ overcame death and justified the sinner.

    e. In His ascension, He has gone to prepare an eternal home for man and to intercede for man.

    f. In His second coming He will take all people He has prepared (who believe in Him) to a place He has prepared for them, a place called eternity with God.

3. **Use your personal testimony**. A great part of your witness is telling them what God has done for you. They may argue with you about the Bible, but few will argue about your personal testimony. A friend of mine, Jim Parker, told me about a time when he was in

college and got a job as a vitamin salesperson. Jim said he stood 6'2" tall but weighed only 135 pounds. He was trying to sell vitamins to a veritable giant. The huge guy asked Jim if he took the vitamins himself. When Jim assured the man he did, the man said, "I don't think I want any of your vitamins; they haven't done anything for you."

4. **Use direct appeal**. Ask a person if he believes. The gospel of Jesus Christ is very personal. Don't beat around the bush; invite the person to Christ (A future section of this book will deal with the invitation). Remember how Paul, when he had finished his message before Agrippa, said, "Agrippa, do you believe the gospel?" (my paraphrase). He made a direct appeal to those who were listening to him.

I believe there were three responses to the message that day.

One, **Festus** told Paul he was out of his mind. You will always have those who consider your message as stupidity.

Two, **Agrippa** put him off. There are many who know the truth, understand the truth, and are impressed by the truth, but because their lifestyle is wrong, and they don't want to give it up, they will put you off until another time. I have wept over a man I loved and shared the gospel with many times. He would come to hear me preach, come out of the service and say with tears in his eyes, "Wayne, don't give up on me." However, to my knowledge he never accepted Jesus as Lord and Savior.

Three, I believe **someone** in that congregation heard and believed, but the Holy Spirit chose not to reveal this to us. I once asked a young man at Antelope Valley Junior College how he came to Christ. He explained that he had eavesdropped on a conversation where one student was explaining the gospel to another—that the Holy Spirit had opened his heart and he prayed to receive Jesus as Lord and Savior. It would be interesting to know if the person who did the witnessing ever knew that he had accepted Christ, and it would also be fascinating to know if the person he was sharing with accepted Christ. Share the gospel. Let God take care of the results.

Another illustration of this third response is an encouragement here. A lady in a northern California town told me she was saved while sitting in her yard by hearing the beautiful music and preaching from an outdoor crusade. She said, "When the evangelist asked people to pray, I did. And Jesus came into my heart. I was so excited that I ran into what I thought to be my house. I heard sounds that I thought were the sounds of angels singing, but then I realized that I had mistakenly run into the chicken house and disturbed them. But I know that Jesus Christ changed my life that night."

Charles G. Finney wrote, "Ordinarily, there are employed in the work of conversion three agents and one instrument. The agents are God, some person who brings the truth to bear on the mind, and the sinner himself. The instrument is the truth of the gospel." While that is ordinary there are exceptions. Finney continued, "There are always two agents, God and the sinner, employed and active in every case of genuine conversion."

Summarizing what Finney had to say about methods, I point out that the agency of God was twofold: God's Providence and His Holy Spirit. God by His Providential government so arranges events as to bring the sinner's mind and the truth into contact. God uses the weather, catastrophe, foreign governments, and who knows what all, to get man's attention. It is then that the gospel can penetrate their minds. This is why I always give an invitation at a funeral meditation, because at the top of the receptivity list is the time of death of a loved one.

Please note how church attendance goes up during times of crisis. I remember some years ago when a major earthquake hit the Los Angeles area. For the next four weeks, attendance spiked in the churches in the Los Angeles area. I asked an elderly Arkansas lady what her thought was on that. She replied, "It's like the old country preacher said, God works in mischievous ways His will to accomplish." Obviously, that was a play on the famous quote: "God uses mysterious ways to accomplish His will."

The Holy Spirit has direct access to the mind, and because He knows the whole history and state of each individual sinner, He employs that truth which is best adapted to his particular case, and then drives it home with Divine power. I have often heard folks testify of a dozen different things God said to different ones of them through a message I had preached with none of those dozen things in mind when I preached. Incidentally, I still believe in door-to-door evangelism, because if one visits about 10 people, God will have at least one prepared to hear the gospel. More on that later.

The agency of people is commonly used by God to bring sinners to Himself. People are active vessels bringing the instrument of the truth to the minds of sinners. Once when a lady was complimenting me on one of my messages, I said, "Thank you, but I am only a vessel." She replied, "Yes, but you are a vessel sent by the Holy Spirit." What a joy to know that God will use us in the conversion of sinners!

The agency of the sinner is seen in that conversion takes place when he obeys the gospel. He is influenced to obey the gospel by God and people. Still, he must surrender his will to God. Therefore, our method is to preach the truth of the gospel, privately and corporately, in the power of the Holy Spirit, that sinners are led to obey the gospel by the influence of the Holy Spirit in their lives and ours. It is not by might of persuasion, nor by power of language that people accept Christ, but by the power of the Holy Spirit. It is God who opens the heart of the sinner to obey the gospel (See the story of Lydia in the Book of Acts: "Whose heart God had opened.")

THE MIGHTY INVITATION OF EVANGELISM (SOLICITATION)

> **MAJOR PREMISE OF**
> **GIVING**
> **INVITATIONS**
> *Revelation 22: 16*
> *Holy Spirit invites*
> *through us*
> *Invitation to come and*
> *take*
> *To those whose*
> *hearts God has*
> *opened*
> *Free to come*

This is the most important point in evangelism...the most important point at the end of a personal presentation of the gospel...the most important point at the end of an evangelistic service is the invitation (a time for people to respond to what they have heard and experienced). When criticized for giving an invitation I respond by pleading guilty--sharing that I am only obeying a command—a command from my Supreme Commander. I tell them that they should not be angry with me for obeying my Master, but angry with themselves for not obeying the gospel.

The major premise for this is found in Revelation 22: 17. There are four things significant. <u>First, it is the Holy Spirit through the church that is making the invitation</u> ("The Spirit and the bride say, "Come.") <u>Second, it is summed up in two words: "come and take"</u>. <u>Third, it is for those whose hearts God has opened</u>: (Whoever has heard the gospel and is thirsty). <u>Fourth, there is no cost to come</u> (take the water of life freely). The major authority for giving invitations is Jesus Christ. His last words to us were that we should get involved in inviting people to come to Him. The last words of the Bible are an invitation to come to Him. I have been severely criticized by people for giving invitations, especially at funerals, harvest festivals, Easter events, musicals, etc. I am oblivious to such criticism. Repeating an important truth, I even try to disarm it by telling people, that if they want to become angry, they should be angry at God, because I am only obeying the instructions of my Supreme Commander.

IF YOU WANT TO BE EFFECTIVE IN EVANGELISM, YOU HAVE TO BE WILLING TO BECOME A FOOL FOR JESUS' SAKE. William Booth of the Salvation Army was told that he looked ludicrous on the street corner playing a tambourine, and persuading people to come to Christ. Booth's reply was, "If it will draw people to Christ, I will get on my hands and knees and crawl up and down the streets."

Is it possible that most churches are declining because they are intimidated about obeying the command of our Lord to invite people to come to Him? Can it be that we are a post-Christian nation because we have been too timid to force the claims of Jesus on a lost world? John R. W. Stott wrote: "We must never make the proclamation without then issuing an appeal...We are to find room for both proclamation and appeal in our preaching if we would be true heralds of the King...It is not enough to teach the gospel; we must urge men to embrace it."

James Stewart wrote: "The sinner is required to hearken and respond to the message or perish. Imbedded in the word "evangelism" is the thought of the messenger waiting to know what answer to take back to Him by whom he was sent. The gospel cannot be ignored. The true evangelist must demand an answer. He cries out like Moses, "I call heaven and earth to record this day against you, that I have set before your life and death, blessing and cursing; therefore, choose life!" (Deuteronomy 30: 19). The messenger of God must not be content merely to preach a delightful sermon. He must breathlessly await the answer to God's ultimatum."

Studying the life of Jesus in the four gospels I find **three key words of invitation** (come, call and follow). Jesus asked more than two dozen times that people come unto Him. For example, consider these: "Come unto Me, all you who are weary and burdened, and I will give you rest. Take my yoke upon you and learn from me…" (Matthew 11: 28ff); "Jesus answered, "If you want to be perfect, go, sell your possessions and give to the poor, and you will have treasure in heaven. Then come, follow me." (Matthew 19: 21); "Come follow Me and I will make you fishers of men." (Mark 1: 17); "If anyone is thirsty, let him come to me and drink." (John 7: 37). At least one-half dozen times Jesus called people to come after Him.

Fifteen (15) times he used the word "follow." One of those was His instructions to the "Rich Young Ruler."

It is clear that Jesus invited people to come to Him. It is also clear that He has commissioned us to invite people to come to Him. Consider the parable of the great banquet as recorded in Luke 14. At the end of the parable we find that many invited guests refused to come, offering three major excuses for not coming (excuses you will have to deal with if your invite people to come to Christ): one said he had some place more important to go (I have just bought a field and I have to go see it—material things placed before God); another said he had something more important to do (I have just purchased a yoke of oxen and I have to try them out—investments placed ahead of God); and, the third said he had someone more important to see (I have just got married—human relationships placed before God).

Embedded in the invitation is the call to repentance. D. L. Moody used to say, "Man is born with his back to God. When he truly repents, he turns around and faces God." David wrote, "I thought on my ways, and turned my feet unto thy testimonies"

(Psalms 119: 59). Derek Prince wrote from his scholarly background: "In his own natural, unregenerate, sinful condition, every man that was ever born has turned his back on God, his Father, and on heaven, his home. In this condition, each step that he takes is a step away from God and from heaven. As he walks this way, the light is behind him and the shadows are before him. The farther he goes, the longer and darker the shadows become. Each step that he takes is one step nearer the end—one step nearer the grave, nearer hell, nearer the endless darkness of a lost eternity. For every man that takes this course, there is one thing that he must do first, one essential act that he must make. He must stop, he must change his mind, change his direction, turn back, turn around, face the opposite way, turn his back to the shadows and face toward the light. The first, essential act is called in the scripture "repentance." It is the first move that any sinner must make who desires to be reconciled with God."

The spiritual gift of exhortation is misused in this modern day. It is used to describe a limited means of encouraging the discouraged. However, in the New Testament the word has a much deeper meaning. R. Alan Streett wrote: "The word "exhort" comes from the Greek word *parakaleo*, used 108 times in the New Testament and variously translated as "beseech," "besought," "exhort," "entreat," and "called." *Parakaleo* (a combination of *para*, "to the side," and *kaleo*, "to call") is used in both classical Greek writings and the New Testament to mean, "to call to one's side, call for, summon."

Corresponding with this writer, Dr. Paige Patterson, president of the Criswell Center for Biblical Studies remarked on *parakaleo:* 'I have frequently translated it as "give an invitation." Any time you come across the word "exhortation" on the pages of the New Testament, you have, in effect, an appeal made for people to come and stand with the speaker in whatever it is that he is doing. This of course could take many patterns, all the way from a silent acquiescence of the heart where one is standing or sitting, to the waving of a hand, or the actual presentation of the person before the congregation. In any case, it is an invitation to decide.'"

Dr. Streett adds, "Seen in this light, *parakaleo* would signify the call for people to come forward and stand by the preacher as an indication of their desire to repent of sin and believe on Jesus Christ...If Dr. Patterson's definition of *parakealo* is correct, Peter actually called for his listeners to respond publicly to his message by presenting themselves to him. The record makes it clear that Peter's invitation elicited an overt response, for approximately three thousand people openly indicated their desire to repent and submit themselves to baptism (v. 41)."

I call the public response a benchmark. How will they know for sure they have decided for Christ unless they make some kind of memorable response—a response that enables them to say to Satan: "Don't try to make me doubt; I was there, and I know that I have taken my stand for Jesus Christ." The former insistence of society to have a public wedding is instructive on this point. Marriage was sacred and precious then. Now, it is no longer considered necessary—just move in together. Is there any wonder why so many relationships break up, since there is no benchmark of commitment? The same may be said concerning church membership—when membership has no meaning or benchmark, many just walk away from an easy commitment.

Consider the parable of Jesus about the invitations to the wedding banquet (Luke 14). Upon the refusals of those invited to come (the Jews), Jesus told His servants to go out quickly (major emphasis on getting outside the church and contacting people in need, as well as the urgency of getting it done today) and bring in **the up-and-outs** (the people in the streets and lanes of the city)—the broken in society (poor, crippled, blind and lame). Note that we are to "bring them in", not just publish invitation fliers.

When the servant reported that he had already done that, Jesus told him to go to **the down-and-outs** of society (the highways and hedges), and make (compel) them to come in. According to W. E. Vine the word "compel" means "to put constraint upon—to constrain, whether by threat, entreaty, force or persuasion." Saul of Tarsus strove to make people blaspheme. Paul, the changed man in Christ, said, "Knowing the terror of the Lord we persuade (Vine says this means "bringing about a change of mind by the influence of reason or moral considerations") people to come to Christ."

Look closely at Vine's definition: Constrain people by *threat*—the threat of eternal hell; by *entreaty*—the joy of forgiveness and eternal life; *force*—the force of the drawing power of the Holy Spirit; and, *persuasion*—the thing that Simon Peter did on the Day of Pentecost. The Bible says that Peter used many other words (describing the length of the invitation)—words of testimony (sharing your own experience or the experiences of others)—and words of exhortation (encouraging—compelling or threatening--people to step across the line for Jesus and identify with Him, taking up their cross and following Him). Go to the last section of this work to find my thought on how to give an effective evangelistic invitation.

THE WHO, WHY, WHAT, WHEN, WHERE AND HOW OF EVANGELISM

FIVE REASONS FOR PERSONAL EVANGELISM

As a follower of Christ, I am under orders

It is essential to personal health and growth

Working with individuals is sound

Accountable to God for how we use our time

A glorious reward awaits those who practice personal evangelism.

WHO is to practice personal evangelism? The Bible gives more instances of the master's personal work than of sermons. He never considered it below His dignity to witness. If we consider personal evangelism below our dignity, we place self above the Master. Anyone really saved should practice personal evangelism. We are saved to bear fruit--to be fruit trees, not shade trees (John 15: 16). There is a seed in each piece of fruit to grow another. Will you go before the Bema judgment seat of Christ with nothing (no other person) in your hands?

WHY is personal evangelism important to me? I will give you **five reasons**.

1. Because I profess to be Christ's follower and am under His command. He says if we follow, He makes us fishers of men (Matthew.4: 19). If I am following

Him, I am fishing. If I am not fishing, I am not following Him. He says, "I will make you..." He can make something of us that we cannot make of ourselves.

2. Personal evangelism is <u>essential to Christian health and growth</u>. Prayer is breath, word is food, witnessing is exercise (For more on this see my book: *"Caring for the Needs of the Newborn Believer"*: Amazon.com). Real happiness is in the obedience of witnessing to the poor, lame, blind, and sick society that is lost in sin.

3. <u>The principle of working with individuals is sound</u>. Insurance sales people use it consistently. According to research by the insurance industry, it takes an average of fourteen months to sell a person a policy. Alcoholics Anonymous works because the person delivered immediately undertakes to deliver another. Mass evangelism is big artillery; personal evangelism is hand-to-hand combat. We cannot reach 1,000 until we reach 1. Reaching one at a time is the best way to reach all in time.

4. <u>We are accountable to God for what we do and how we spend our time</u>. 2 Corinthians 5: 10: "For we must all appear before the tribunal of Christ, so that each may be repaid for what he has done in the body, whether good or worthless." Romans 14: 12: "So then, each of us will give an account of himself to God." Matthew 12: 36: "I tell you that on the day of judgment people will have to account for every careless word they speak."

5. <u>A glorious reward awaits disciple winners in the next life</u>. In the parable of the vineyard owner (Matthew.25: 14-30) we find how each person gives a report to the Master. Please notice that it took only 12 words to give a good account. On the other hand, it took 40 words (more than three times as many words) to give an excuse. To the two slaves who brought a good report, the Master made a promise—a promise of glorious reward: "Well done, good and faithful slave! You were faithful over a few things; I will put you in charge of many things. Share your Master's joy!" To the one who was unfaithful, what was his was taken and given to someone who

would be faithful, and he was cast out.

WHAT keeps people from witnessing for Christ? They want people to know their extraordinary friends, why not Christ? I will list four things:

a. They have no genuine experience of Christ. He is not real to them. They have no fellowship with Him (devotional life). People want to know what we know by experience.

b. They have sins known to them that they have harbored in their lives. Known sin paralyzes a person because of the fear he will be found out. Some deny (lie about it) they have known sins (1 John 1: 6). Others tell the lie so long they become deceived into believing they have no sin (1 John 1: 8). Still others continue the downward spiral and call God a liar about their sins, saying that there is nothing wrong with their wrong. (1 John 1: 10). The solution to this is so simple and is found in verse 9 of 1 John 1: "If we confess our sins, He is faithful and righteous to forgive us our sins and to cleanse us from all unrighteousness."

c. They are intimidated by fear. They fear their lack of ability, not realizing that fear is not from God but from Satan (2 Timothy 1: 6-8: "Therefore, I remind you to keep ablaze the gift of God that is in you through the laying on of my hands. For God has not given us a spirit of fearfulness, but one of power, love, and sound judgment. So, don't be ashamed of the testimony about our Lord, or of me His prisoner. Instead, share in suffering for the gospel, relying on the power of God.")

d. They have no concern for lost souls. No tears, no souls (See Psalm 126: 5-6). Concern comes by doing. Fact—Faith—Feeling (Bill Bright). You act upon the facts of the gospel by faith; then comes the feeing. You act upon the facts of people being lost, witness to them by faith; then comes the feeling of concern.

Several things are important in this passage. First, *zeal for personal witnessing naturally dies out*—it must be deliberately fanned to keep it ablaze. Second, *fear does not come from God*. Instead, He gives power to deal with our weaknesses and the resistance of the lost. He gives love to deal with the unlovely and un-loveable of society. He gives us sound thinking to deal with the perplexing questions or objections that those to whom we witness give us. Third, *we are to never be ashamed of testifying about our Lord*. We must settle the question of our minds, namely, is God able to save anyone, even the dregs of society? Fourth, *we are to be willing to be embarrassed, or even suffer, for sharing the gospel*. Fifth, *we are to rely on God's power* ("Not by power or by might, but by My Spirit, says the Lord).

Under this section, let's analyze the cause of fear (the lack of courage). We are confused on major issues, which confusion stops us from personal evangelism. Following are some questions we entertain that cause us to fear to share the gospel.

1. "Am I good enough to begin to share the gospel? Am I advanced far enough?" As can be seen, we are not speaking of being righteous enough. That has been settled by the righteousness of Christ in us. We are speaking of the fear of being so new that we don't know how or have the proper information to share. The answer: we cannot wait until we are perfect—that is like waiting until we can afford children. We gain knowledge by teaching—the teacher always learns more than the student. God gets glory from our infirmities. We can all share what happened to us. Like the man healed from blindness, we can say, "I don't know all the answers, but one thing I do know—I was blind and now I see."

2. "What if I fail? I don't want to be embarrassed." That is pride. We are far too enamored with success over faithfulness. Faithfulness is success. We cannot win anyone; we can only witness to them. The Holy Spirit is the only soul-winner in the universe. Share the good news in His power and leave the results in His capable hands.

3."Is there no danger of doing more harm than good?" No! Unequivocally, No! This is the lie of Satan. He knows how effective personal evangelism is. "Must I always talk to everyone all the time?" No, but we are to try to open doors (See the section on Intentional Evangelism for further instruction here).

4. How can I talk to people when they have no interest?" If they are not interested in your concern for them, win them over by being interested in their concern (I repeat a popular line: "People don't care how much we know until they know how much we care"). Love them (i.e. have an unselfish concern for their good), and approach their interests, asking the Holy Spirit to open the door for a witness.

5. "How can I try personal evangelism when I do not love people?" Human love is an affection of feeling. Godly love is a decision. The concern or passion and love will come as you do it. Remember the little train: Fact>Faith>Feeling (Bill Bright).

6. "Dare I begin this work when I know so little about the Bible?" Again, we learn by doing. Again, the Holy Spirit will call to your mind what you need to say. You can also be honest and say, "I don't know the answer to that, but here is what I do know." The best student is he who knows he doesn't know. Witness and study at the same time. I have learned more from lost people than I have in conferences or clinics on disciple winning. In other words, just do it, and, as a result, the knowledge will come.

7. "How can I help people when I cannot answer all their questions?" This was what Satan tried with the woman at the well of Sychar. He got her to argue about denominations. Jesus gently drew her back to the main subject. You can say, "That's an interesting question. I don't know the answer, but I will jot that down and try to answer that later. Let's talk for now about what I know."

PRINCIPLES IN PERSONAL WITNESSING

1. **Don't lose your temper**. Keep amicable. Don't chase rabbits. Stay focused on the gospel. I once asked a person if I could share the gospel with him. He replied, "Yes, but I have a thousand questions." I said, "Okay! I will try to answer your questions, but first, let me share the gospel with you." He agreed. About 30 minutes later as we sat rejoicing in his profession of faith in Jesus Christ, I said, "Okay, what is your first question?" He said, "I cannot remember any questions right now." I said, "That is because Jesus is the answer. When you accepted Him, He became your Lord, Savior and answer."

2. **Avoid arguments**. Tell them this matter is a lifetime pursuit...that some questions are too difficult for us. Again, like the blind man who was healed, you can honestly say, "I don't know, but one thing I do know."

3. **Let your conversation be salty**. Colossians 4: 6: "Your speech should always be gracious, seasoned with salt, so that you may know how you should answer each person." Salt makes things more palatable. It preserves what is said. It is an antidote to corruption. It enhances flavor.

4. WHERE can personal evangelism be done? The simple answer is: **wherever God opens the door**. I have witnessed in church, on the street, at sports events, in saloons and bars, on airplanes, in the market-place, most anywhere. It can be done in sermons, in teaching, but these are limited to certain places. Begin where you are. Not only should you look for opportunities, but you should try to create them. (For more on this, refer to the section on Intentional Evangelism).

5. Here is a proper place to say a word about **how to get into a home**. There are several things to consider:

a. <u>Have something to identify you from those who habitually knock on doors to spread their message</u>. If they assume that you are one of those two particular groups, they are likely to turn you away. A church bulletin or a tract with the name of your church on it will suffice.

b. <u>Use the direct approach</u>—tell them exactly who you are and why you are there. You may say something like: "Hello, my name is _____. I am from the _____ Church. Your child is in our Bible study program (mission group, youth group, tutoring program, etc.). I wanted to come by and get acquainted with the parents of my pupils. May I come in and visit for a few moments? If not now, when would be a good time to come back? (Set a time and keep your appointment). Or, "Hello, my name is _____. I am from the _____ Church. I wanted to come by and let you know that we are in the community praying for the needs of the folks in our area. Is there anything you need prayer about at this time? If you need time, I will be happy to visit in your home now or at a later time. When is an appropriate time?" Another approach could begin like this: "Hello, my name is _____ from the _____ Church. We are happy you decided to visit in our church. I wanted to get acquainted. May I come in for a few minutes?" Still another approach: "Hello, my name is _____. I am visiting in the community to find out what kind of church people would like to attend. What would you look for in a church you would like to attend? May I come in and visit to determine how to meet your desires in a church?"

Personal Evangelism Technique: Please refer back to the section, METHOD OF EVANGELISM, as well as INTENTIONAL EVANGELISM. **Ask someone who is experienced in witnessing to accompany him or her and watch.** Attend a conference on personal witnessing. Read a good book on the subject, but don't just read. Practice what you read. I have never taken a formal golf lesson, but I have read Golf Magazine on the course, applying what I just read. That is the way I have learned to play golf. ABOVE ALL, ASK THE HOLY SPIRIT TO TEACH YOU. When you ask Him to teach you, remember that He doesn't teach in isolation. He will teach you as you try to share.

THE PERSONAL WITNESS HIMSELF

I will answer three questions, along with some instruction on how to start the conversation and draw to a conclusion. The three questions are: What must a witness be? What must a witness have? What must a witness know?

WHAT HE MUST BE. Initially, I point out that he is an instrument in God's plans and hands, and, therefore, needs to be an instrument God can use. There are only three instruments in personal evangelism: WORD—HOLY SPIRIT—PERSONAL WITNESS. The Word and the Spirit are constant (never-changing); the Personal Witness is the changing one.

1. The personal witness should be saved and sure of it. 2 Timothy 1:12: "But I am not ashamed, because I know the One, I have believed in and am persuaded that He is able to guard what has been entrusted to me until that day." We commend Christ by what we know. How can one know Christ? Confess, believe and receive. For more assurance study John 10, Romans 8, 1 John (entire book: I have a commentary, not yet printed, on 1 John. It lists about 20 solid proofs that one is saved), Colossians 3:3, and Jude 24-25.

2. The personal witness should live a consistent and clean life. He doesn't want the devil to discredit his testimony (throw his testimony out of court because of untrustworthiness). "The church is looking for better methods, but God is looking for better men." (Author unknown). Doctors use clean instruments—so does God. God doesn't demand perfect instruments, but He does demand clean

ones. Purification comes before power (See Psalms 51 and 32).

3. The personal witness should be <u>wholly yielded and surrendered to the Lord</u>. Consider the lad with the loaves and fishes in John 11. Someone wittingly said, "There were two miracles that day. First, that he hadn't already eaten his lunch, and second, that Jesus could take so little and feed so many." It wasn't much he had, but when he gave it to the Lord it was multiplied, and he still had as much to eat after his meal had fed over 5,000 others. So, can God multiply your "little". His strength is made perfect in our weakness.

4. The personal witness needs to be <u>filled with the Holy Spirit</u>. Zechariah 4:4 says, "Not by might and not by power, but by my Spirit, says the Lord." We know stories of how great musicians helped small children play great works by covering the mistakes of the child. So, the Holy Spirit will cover your mistakes.

5. The personal witness must be <u>a person of prayer</u>. We cannot pray for a lost person without witnessing to them; we cannot witness to them without praying for them. Two parts to witnessing: going to God for sinners and going to sinners for God. There are four things for which to pray: ask God to bring us into contact with the right persons; ask Him to give us the right words to say; ask that He speak through you by the Holy Spirit; and, ask Him to carry on the work after we are gone. Wait on the Lord.

God has taught me much about prayer, and I am still learning. I was in Teague, South Korea. I was scheduled to speak to a school of junior high boys (9,500 students). The only place for an assembly that large was a red clay soccer field, but it was the monsoon season in Teague, and it was raining. I gathered my team and we prayed: "Lord, we know the farmers need the rain, but we believe that 9,500 souls needing to hear the gospel is sufficient reason to ask you to stop   the rain. In Jesus name, we thank you for making it so."

We went to bed. The wind changed, and the rain ceased. The wind dried out the field, so, we could assemble. I gave the invitation, prayed with the students, and asked those who had prayed to receive Christ to stand to their feet. 6,500 immediately stood to their feet. Knowing the polite nature and syncretistic nature of the Koreans (the Koreans were like the Athenians, wanting to cover all the bases and erecting a statue to the "unknown god"), I said, "Wait a minute. Sit back down. I want you to know that I am asking you to forsake all other gods and accept Jesus Christ as your only Lord and Savior. Now, all of you who will reject all other gods and accept Jesus Christ as your Lord and Savior, please stand to your feet."

Once again, 6,500 stood to their feet (I will share a very personal story with you in another place about this incident). After giving them the follow-up materials and instructing them on the importance of baptism and church attendance, we closed the meeting. My wife and I went to the principal's office and had tea. He thanked us for coming and we left. I opened the door of the taxi car and let my wife in. I went to the other side of the taxi car. As I lifted my right foot to get into the taxi car, it started to pour rain, and rained for the next several days.

WHAT HE MUST HAVE

Love—for the Lord and for lost people. Someone said, "Have a cool head and a hot heart." Love leads to untiring effort to win people to Christ. Love attracts lost people to us. We obtain this kind of love by dwelling on Christ's love for us, and by asking the Holy Spirit to impart this love to us. Romans 5:5 says, "This hope will not disappoint us, because God's love has been poured out in our hearts through the Holy Spirit who was given to us." The more yielded we are to Him, the more love we have for lost people around us. This love is more an intellectual concern for the good of another than it is a feeling of sympathy. It is poured out into the heart of the Spirit-filled believer. The Holy Spirit does the pouring out (not just a dripping); we do the actions of love (meeting ministry needs, sharing words of concern and words of the gospel). Since God loves us at all times, but doesn't always like what we do, we can also love people we don't like. As we follow through on acts of love, we will find out that we begin to love them.

I promised earlier to share a very personal story with you. Here it is. It involves a story my mother told me on the day I was ordained by the New Palestine Baptist Church in Picayune, Mississippi—a day which by God's providence was my father and mother's 38th wedding anniversary. I'll never forget that day for two reasons, one silly and the other quite emotional.

The silly reason was that when the ordaining council had finished questioning me for over 2 hours, my pastor asked if there were any more questions. When no one came forward with another question, my pastor asked me what the last thing was I needed to do before I went into the pulpit. I thought along the lines of: go over my notes, say another brief prayer, think of my first words, etc. Finally, I told him I didn't know. He then gave me the answer: "Make sure your trousers are zipped."

The emotional part goes back to my earliest recollections. I have always known that God wanted me to preach the gospel. I knew that long before I was saved. I can remember as a child gathering our dogs into a covered canopy from an army cart and preaching to them. I also remember taking them down to the pond and baptizing them. Maybe that sounds ridiculous to you, but it was serious to me. Even in those days if someone asked what I would do when I grew up, I would tell them I was going to preach the gospel. I didn't know until my ordination why I knew that. My mother never told me this story until my ordination day.

I am the seventh of nine children. My mother, according to her story, was physically in no shape to bear me because of sickness. Her doctor told her she had two choices: either give me up (nice phrase for abort me) and live to take care of the six children she had or give birth to me and have someone else take care of the seven children.

My mother turned her face to the wall in prayer. She told God she couldn't believe in abortion—that she was willing to die to give me birth—but if He could   see fit to please give her strength to birth me and still bring up all seven. Whether she was right to do so, she bargained with God. In those days there was no sure way to determine the sex of a child until birth. She told God that if He heard her prayer and gave her such strength that, if I was a male child, she would dedicate me to preach the gospel. I'll never forget her words: "I have kept this a secret for 22 years because I wanted to make sure you were God-called and not mother-called." I am certain that God called me. I well remember my fig tree experience. As I was gathering the figs, God spoke to my heart the following words: "Follow Me, and I will make you a gatherer of men." Though I diligently sought the best education I could get, I believe it is God who "made me" a preacher. My education enhanced my abilities, but it was God who gave them to me.

That takes me back to Teague, South Korea, when I spoke at the junior high school. Knowing that my mother grew up in a hyper-Calvinistic church, and that they had told her when she announced that God wanted her to be a missionary, "Girls can't go, and God will save them in His own way," she could not go as a missionary. So, when those 6,500 young men gave their hearts to the Lord, I found myself on my face behind the podium, saying, "God, please put those on my mother's account, so that at her bema judgment, she can have some trophies to present before your feet." I firmly believe that God's way of her being a missionary was through me. And I praise Him for it.

Courage—cowards have no convictions. Without convictions there is no concern. If we are not convinced there is a hell to be endured or a heaven to be enjoyed, we will have very little concern for people's destination. Courage is indispensable to every leader. People say it is so hard to love people. Is it hard to pull a drowning person from the water? Joshua 1: 9: "Haven't I commanded you: be strong and courageous? Do not be afraid or discouraged, for the Lord your God is with you wherever you go." Proverbs 29: 25: "The fear of man is a snare, but the one who trusts in the Lord is protected." 2 Timothy 1: 7 indicates that fear is not from God, but, in the place of fear, we are given power, love and a sound mind.

Tact and wisdom. A battle is often won or lost in the way we approach people. Be prayerful. Be careful. Be courteous. Colossians 4: 6: Your speech should always be gracious, seasoned with salt, so that you may know how you should answer each person."

Patience—perseverance. Personal evangelism requires more patience than any spiritual work. Strike "I can't" from your personal vocabulary. In the context concerning the resurrection of our bodies we find the concluding remark to be: "Therefore, my dear brothers, be steadfast, immovable, always excelling in the Lord's work, knowing that your labor in the Lord is not in vain." Someone wrote: "Most anything we do in this life is vanity (Ecclesiastes. 1: 2-3), but labor in the Lord has eternal value."

Faith—faith in God and faith in His Word. God still works miracles. Don't doubt like Sarah or Thomas. Just believe. Love the Word, live the Word, believe the Word, memorize the Word, and go out and sow the seed of the Word. 1 Peter 1: 20-21: "He (Jesus) was chosen before the foundation of the world but was revealed at the end of the times for you who through Him are believers in God, who raised Him from the dead and gave Him glory, so that your faith and hope are in God." Don't trust in your ability, but in God. If we do the work of sowing, He will do the work of growing, so that we may do the work of reaping.

Have faith in the power of the gospel. I was in Pusan, South Korea. There was a major prison there, a prison for the worst of criminals (a maximum security prison). I asked the missionary if he could get us an opportunity to speak to these men. He said he couldn't and that we best spend our time on people who would be likely to receive our message. I asked him if he had ever tried to get into the prison. When he said he hadn't, I told him, "With all due respect, I am going to go around you and try to get in there with the gospel." It turned out that the warden was a Christian. He told me that he could not assemble the prisoners, but that I could preach over the intercom system and visit those who desired in the hallways outside their cells. We preached the gospel and gave an invitation. Out of about 2,500 prisoners over 2,100 let us pray with them and leave them our follow-up materials. I am content to leave the results in God's hands.

WHAT HE MUST KNOW

He must know and be fully convinced that people outside of Christ are lost and on their way to hell. The picture Jesus painted of lostness in Luke 15 is vivid: some people, like the sheep, are lost by their appetites; some, like the coin, are lost because of inability; some, like the younger son, are lost by actions; and, some, like the older son, are lost by attitudes. The Bible not only paints people as lost without Christ, but also blind to spiritual things of life and values (See 2 Cor. 4: 3,4), and "dead in trespasses and sins" (See Eph. 2: 1, 5).

He needs to know the content of the gospel. The summary statement of the gospel is found in 1 Corinthians 15: 1-11. The salient points are that Christ died for our sins (in our place), He was buried to endure hell for us, He was raised to life for our justification and to guarantee our resurrection, and this was testified by many witnesses. That was His part. Our part is to believe unto salvation and be steadfast in our spiritual journey. As one grows in his knowledge of the gospel, he will find more than a dozen concepts that clarify the gospel—words such as redemption, justification, forgiveness, sanctification, glorification, etc. I recommend for further study on this to see the previous section where I summarize the works of Louis Sperry Chafer and/or H.L. Wilmington (Go back and review my section on "Soteriology").

The personal witness must know and be convinced that Jesus is the only way one can be saved (See John 14: 6: He is the way—every other way is wrong; He is the life—any other effort is death; He is the truth—anything else is a lie). Acts 4: 12: "Neither is there salvation in any other, for there is no other name under heaven given among men by which we must be saved." I repeat: There may be many ways to the cross, but the cross is the only way to heaven. C.H. Spurgeon met a scoffer on the streets of London one day. The scoffer yelled across the street, "Hey! Mr. Spurgeon. How does a person get to heaven?" Without missing a stride Spurgeon answered, "My friend, go to the cross, turn right and go straight."

He needs to know the work and place of the Holy Spirit and the Word in conversion. Faith comes by hearing, and hearing by the Word of God—His Word is much more important than our words. So, the Word is the instrument; the personal witness is the means of transmission of the Word, and the Holy Spirit takes the Word, drives it home to the human heart, opens the heart, and enables the person to believe unto salvation.

He must know the best Bible passages that will lead people to faith in Christ. Anyone can memorize if they apply themselves to it. Know the Word in your heart and share the Word with your mouth. God will do the miraculous and bring about the new birth. Once when I was sharing the gospel accompanied by a Korean pastor on the streets of Seoul, South Korea, we stopped in a game room where a large group of older men were playing some Korean board games. I tried several approaches, but they just ignored me and kept playing their games. I uttered a prayer under my breath: "God, how can I get these men to listen?" Immediately, from my mouth came these words: "Hey! Guys! I went to Buddha's shrine today. I noticed that he had ears but couldn't hear me. He had eyes but couldn't see me; arms but couldn't support me; legs but couldn't walk with me; and a mouth but couldn't talk to me" (a paraphrase of two Psalms). Now, I had their full attention, because it is God's words (Scripture), and not my words that have power. For the next 20 minutes, through my interpreter, I spoke to them of the living God, who can see, hear, speak, support and accompany them. I have no knowledge if any of them became Christians. But I do know that God's Word is powerful when used in sharing about God.

HOW TO START THE CONVERSATION

Knowing all of these things, how can one start the conversation concerning them? Questions are an excellent way. Ask about the person, and you will discover a jumping-off place to change the conversation to Christ. Here are a couple of my favorite questions and how to get started on the interview: What's the greatest thing that has ever happened to you? Listen carefully and commend them. Then say, "May I share with you the greatest thing that has ever happened to me?" Share your testimony and ask if that happened to them.

A similar question is, "Who is the greatest person you ever met?" Use the same approach, listening and commending. Then ask if you can share the greatest person you ever met, introducing Christ as that person.

Here's another: "What are your plans for the future?" Let them share, then ask, "What then?" Keep asking the "what then" until you get to death. Show them the answer to death is eternal life through Jesus Christ.

The direct approach is: "I have started this conversation with you because I am concerned for you and I wanted you to know what Christ has done in my life and what He wants to do in your life." If you sense resistance at any point, simply say, "I sense that you are not ready to talk about these things right now. Perhaps we can have another time to talk. Would that be okay?" God does not push Himself on people; He invites. Neither should we try to push Him onto people; we should invite them to Him and leave the results in His hands. (Note: if they indicate it is okay to talk to them about Jesus Christ, proceed using words "seasoned with salt."

Sharing your testimony in a brief form (about 1 to ½ minutes) is an excellent way to get into the interview. In order to do this, you need to write it out. Use these four questions as an outline to write your testimony: what I was before I met Christ; how I realized my problem; how I came to know Christ; and, what being a Christian means to me now that I am saved. Most people will not argue with your testimony. Most will listen to your testimony if you keep it short and simple, avoiding churchy words.

HOW TO PRESS FOR A DECISION

Again, using questions is helpful—questions like: do you understand what it means to make Jesus your Lord? Do you have questions that I can clarify? Are you ready to ask Jesus to come into your life? (If yes, show him how you prayed, assuring him that prayer doesn't save, but it does indicate a desire to be saved). Suggest a prayer, one sentence at a time, asking him to put the prayer into his own words. Once he has prayed, ask him if he was sincere. If he says he was, ask him where Jesus Christ in relation to him is. If he indicates that Jesus has come into his heart, welcome him as your brother (sons of the same heavenly Father). Instruct him on further steps such as baptism and church attendance, prayer and Bible reading, and fellowship with the family (the church). If he indicates "no" at any point, ask if he still has questions. If not, thank him for letting you share, assuring him that you will pray that God will open his heart. End the conversation congenially.

FAITHFUL NOT SUCCESSFUL

Faithfulness is success. Jesus told us to expect that when we sow gospel seeds, we will encounter four kinds of soil (See Mark 4: 3-20). There will be soil like concrete. The birds will eat seed and it will never grow (Non-conversion); there will be shallow soil where there appears to be success but the plant withers and dies (emotional conversion); there will be rocky and thorny soil where the weeds crowd out the good seed (no repentance resulting in intellectual conversion); finally, there will be good soil and the plant will grow and produce a crop (spiritual conversion). Only God knows for sure—we don't. One more time: Share the gospel in the power of the Holy Spirit and leave the results in the hands of God. When you do you are successful.

BASIC PRINCIPLES OF EVANGELISM EXPLAINED

EVANGELISM THE PROBLEM SOLVER

Evangelism can solve any problem that a church may have. These are neither the motives nor the goals for evangelism but the results of evangelism. Let me mention a few problems a church can have and show you how evangelism can solve them.

1. Lack of finances—win more people to help share the financial load.

2. Fights in the church—my brother and I fought each other every day, but if someone else tried to whip one, he had to whip both. We had a common foe. When we win souls, we are fighting Satan. He is our common foe and fighting him draws us together. An ancient proverb says, "Whoever is an enemy of my enemy is my friend."

3. Lack of leadership—Win and train new leadership. Most preachers and missionaries come out of evangelistic churches.

4. Lack of faith—when we see people walking the aisles for Jesus, we believe God in a stronger way.

5. Lack of prayer—we cannot be concerned about those to whom we have witnessed without praying for them; we cannot pray for them without witnessing to them.

Too much or too little space—too much space can be filled by reaching more people. Too little space can be solved by reaching more people who will help build more space.

6. Sinfulness—before we can do evangelism, we must be clean; doing it requires that we stay clean.

LESSONS FROM THE PERSONALITY SCALE

> *Not necessarily large*
> *Necessarily growing*

I want to make a disclaimer at this point. I do not believe that every church has to be large, while I do believe each church should seek to grow. There is room and need for all sizes of churches. This is true because each of us is subject to a scale—a scale that has relationship at the left side and project at the right side. Some people will sacrifice projects to protect relationships; others will sacrifice relationships to protect projects. It is probable that one should not try to operate outside his place on that scale. Only Jesus was right in the middle.

Also, each church has strengths and weaknesses regardless of its size. A small church can train up young leaders more effectively in that it can use them in capacities that the large church cannot. When I was 15, I was the principal of the summer Vacation Bible School in my small rural church. The big churches in town could not get away with that. However, that, along with other things, prepared me for the ministry that God had for me. On the other hand, I did not have a youth pastor because my church could not afford to have that staff position—said youth pastor of the large church investing in me what the small church invested.

CAUTIONS ABOUT THE PERSONALITY SCALE

PERSONALITY SCALE

Relational_____

Jesus_____

Project Oriented

Relational will sacrifice the project for the relationship; project oriented will sacrifice the relationship for the project. Only Jesus had the perfect balance.

One should not criticize the other, but each should strive toward the balance Jesus had.

---

1. **The scale represents a general tendency, not a fixed action predictor**. Even though Jesus was able to be central on the scale, balancing projects and relationships, He varied from them at times. For example: When He was going to Jerusalem to face the cross, He was project oriented ("He set His face like a flint). On the other hand, He could be toward the extreme relational side as well. For example: He wept over Jerusalem; His bowels moved with compassion toward the people who were scattered like sheep without a shepherd; and, He wept at the tomb of Lazarus.

2. **Circumstances can affect where we are on the sc**ale. Let's use Paul and Barnabas as our examples of the scale. When arguing over whether to take John Mark along on another missionary journey, Paul took the extreme side of being project oriented. I can almost hear him saying something like this: "No way, am I taking that panty-waist again. He'll get out there and get homesick when the going gets tough and want to go back home as he did before." Barnabas took the extreme side of being relationship oriented. I can

almost hear him say something like: "Now, Brother Paul, calm down. Don't you remember how I had to introduce you to the church to get you accepted. I'm sure John Mark will learn from his mistakes."

3. **Spiritual growth can cause us to alter our point on the scale**. Paul, for example, when he was in the cold, dark, dank pit of a prison, could write: "Demas has deserted me because he loved this present world, and has gone to Thessalonica. Crescens has gone to Galatia, Titus to Dalmatia. Only Luke is with me. Bring Mark with you for he is useful to me in the ministry." (2 Timothy 4: 10-11). Here we see that Paul was wrong about two people: To Demas he was close in relationship, but Demas let him down; to John Mark he was distanced because of his project, but John Mark surprised him, even penning one of the Four Gospels.

4. **God uses people no matter where they are on the scale**. Barnabas was hindering the missionary journey (project) that the Holy Spirit had laid on Paul's heart. However, he raised up another young man to accompany him on a different ministry. Yet, Barnabas was right about John Mark. Paul, on the other hand, had a very successful missionary journey.

5. **All of us will at some point wish we had intensified on the project side**, because we let a relationship affect a decision that needed to be made. I had a very dear friend who had a great church die under him because he was too relational to a small group, letting them cloud his judgment concerning moving ahead with the greater part of the congregation. On the other hand, all of us at another point wish we had modified on the relationship side, because we so wounded a person who might have made a great contribution to the ministry of our Lord Jesus Christ. I will regret until my dying day how I treated a person on one of my teams wounding him deeply, because that person was questioning my project.

6. **The only way to adjust rightly on the scale is to be filled with the Holy Spirit**. Find out where God is moving and join Him (See Blackaby's *Experiencing God*), and He will take care of the people

around you. Pray through every decision and follow the leading of the Holy Spirit through the confirmation of Scripture (i.e. make sure you have a *rhema* from the Lord).

REASONS FOR ALL SIZE CHURCHES

> **Reasons for all sizes of churches**
>
> Preference of relationships
>
> All types of ministers
>
> Deferring population bases

In addition to the scale, there are three reasons we need all sizes of churches:

(1) Many people prefer a relational church, while others prefer a project-oriented church, and all places on the scale in between these two.

(2) many pastors prefer a relational church, while others prefer a project-oriented church with all places on the scale in between

(3) many places do not have the population necessary for a large church, while many places within a large population do not fit the necessities to grow a large church.

There are statements that need to be made in relation to this scale idea.

(1) No one should look down on a small church because his is large.

(2) no one should criticize or be jealous toward the large church because his is small.

(3) no one should feel smug because he is a small church

(relational) pastor, using that as an excuse to avoid intentional evangelism.

(4) no one should feel smug because he is a large church (project-oriented) pastor, using that as a basis to boast of his intentional evangelism or to cover up his lack thereof.

(5) we all need to rejoice in every size church, because we need thousands more of all size churches.

This means that we should be supportive of all sizes, praying for all sizes, commending all sizes, and planting all sizes. The small church pastor should be planting more churches, and the large church pastor should be planting more churches (Statistical data shows that new church plants grow more rapidly than small ones). Each size church should be using the methodology that best suits it to train up new leaders (call out the called).

EVANGELISM EQUALS JESUS KNOWN AND MADE KNOWN

In Matthew 16: 13-16 we are shown that Christ is known only by the revelation of the Holy Spirit and must be made known in the same way. The passage also gives us **three major thoughts**:

1. It tells us where the hope of evangelism lies

2. it tells us how the church is to carry out its task

3. it tells us what happens when the church gives its answer to who Jesus is.

Most people agree that the greatest need of our churches today is to increase our evangelistic thrust, but how to do it is quite another matter. Some of us have become so frustrated about it that we have gone to extreme measures to try to promote evangelism. There is a story called "The Gospel Blimp." It is an apt description of an extreme measure. This group of people became concerned for a next door neighbor. They became so concerned that they bought a blimp, organized an association, spent thousands of dollars carrying signs over the city, added a loud speaker and even preached over the air (literally), including dropping gospel tracts from the blimp. After three years they had spent thousands of dollars, caused innumerable problems, and ended away from their original purpose, and the gospel blimp had not won the man and his wife to Christ. However, the other next door neighbor had won the man and his wife to Christ by being a friend to them and helping them in their time of need.

Where is the hope of evangelism? Does it lie in junking all the old ideas? Does it lie in dreaming up new ideas? Paul certainly had the answer when he said, "I am become all things to all men that I might thereby win some."

Evangelism is not **repeating a formula**. One person told me he led over a hundred to faith in Christ during the lunch hour as he witnessed at a busy intersection. He could have done no more than get them to agree to a formula.

Evangelism is not necessarily **coming forward in church**. Those who come forward usually need to be led to make a decision for Christ. It is imperative that we do more than have them fill out a decision card and dunk them in the baptistery. Many have come forward and received no counsel as to how to make a decision for Christ. I believe this is one of the major reasons we have so many whose names are on church rolls, yet their lives have not been changed.

Evangelism is not an **agreement that a Scripture is right**. The devils believe the Bible is true (See James 2: 19), but they are not saved. Even the devil can quote (misquote) Scripture, and we know his destiny.

Evangelism is not **winning an argument**. Some of us are better debaters than others. Let me caution us all that we can win an argument and lose a soul. Jesus didn't set out to win arguments. He set out to change people from the inside out.

Not repeating a formula
Not necessarily coming forward in a church meeting
Not an agreement of a certain Scripture
Not winning an argument

Evangelism is presenting Christ in the power of the Holy Spirit to the unbeliever and persuading him to be born again. How shall we get that job done? That leads to the next issue...the issue of where the hope of evangelism lies.

WHERE THE HOPE OF EVANGELISM LIES

Note where it does not lie:

1. It does not lie in the DENOMINATION. The denomination is doing a wonderful thing by teaching witnessing classes, and you would do well to have one in your church, but if evangelism is not done by the local congregation who can win, baptize, nourish and teach, it will not be done. I am a church man. Although I travel the world doing evangelism, I believe that the task of all evangelism must come back to the local congregation.

2. The hope does not lie in EXPERIMENTAL CHURCHES. We certainly can learn some things form these churches. Being an evangelist, I believe in area-wide crusades, local church revivals, coffee house ministries, street ministries, resort ministries, etc. In short, I believe in most of the new and innovative methods of evangelism. It is true that we are not getting lost people to attend the local church. Only three out of one hundred persons in attendance at the average church are unchurched, whereas in area-wide crusades, etc. we get up to forty-five out of a hundred who are

unchurched. However, when persons are reached, they must be enrolled in a local church. Let every evangelist be cautioned and instructed that there is no success in any of these innovative ideas without the support of the local churches. An evangelist who "kicks" the church is like the proverbial dog that bites the hand that feeds it.

3. The hope of evangelism does not lie in bringing into the church PROGRAMS THAT COMPETE WITH WHAT THE WORLD HAS TO OFFER. I am all for recreation programs, entertainment rooms in the church building, etc..., if they can be utilized to reach people. However, before you rush off to change your structure or to knock out a partition, remember this: Because we are different than the world, and because we have something, indeed SOMEONE, special to offer, we had better offer people that SOMEONE that the world cannot offer. We cannot compete with the world at its own game. The churches had better stick to the game plan that Jesus left us, a game plan that is given in detail in the Bible. The church was not put here to compete with the world, but to change the world.

Note where the hope of evangelism lies: It lies in the church...the local church (not the church building, but the people who make up the church). Whenever the church is first mentioned in the New Testament it is mentioned in connection with evangelism. In Matthew 16: 18 Jesus says, "I will build my church" upon Peter and such men as are like Peter. The invisible, spiritual church is built upon Jesus Christ, but the visible, physical church is built upon people...people who have confessed what Peter confessed, namely, that Jesus Christ is the Savior of the world, the Son of the Living God. It is first Christ, the root, then the church, the outgrowth; first, Christ, the builder, then the church, which is His building. The most important question is not, "To which part of the church do you belong?" Instead, it is, "Do you belong to Jesus Christ, the son of the Living God?" And this must be decided by the other question, "Whom do you say that I Am?" It is very significant that our Lord should connect with the church the right idea of Himself. Here is the question which must be put to everyone who is to be admitted into the assembly of the Lord…" Whom say ye that I am?" That is the primary task of the church…to confront people with the question, "Who do you think Jesus is?" That is evangelism.

HOW IS THE CHURCH TO CARRY OUT ITS TASK?

1. THE CHURCH MUST HAVE SOME FOUNDATIONS.

World's answers are diverse

World's answers contradict Christ

World's answers don't agree

World's answers are generally respectful

World's answers are wrong

World's answers are unblessed

a. We need to recover A WORSHIP OF THE LIVING GOD THAT IS EXCITING, or we will not be able to do the task of evangelism. Boring services drive people away rather than entice them to return. We need to return to a fellowship of love in the life of the church. In a world that is full of so much hatred, we need a haven where there is trust and concern. We also need a renewal of the study of the Word of God. The average person does not know what the Bible has to say. How can he minister to a NEEDY WORLD?

2. THE CHURCH MUST ANSWER THE QUESTION, *WHO IS CHRIST?*

The church's answer to the question, "Who is Christ?" must be different from the answer the world gives. Jesus challenged the Twelve Disciples with this question: "Who do men say that I, the Son of Man am?" He also challenged Nicodemus that in order to be born again he had to change his view of who Jesus is.

3. WHAT DOES THE WORLD SAY?

a. What does the world say about Jesus? I will make six statements concerning this: a) The answers of the world are DIVERSE. "A thousand lies will live together and tolerate each other. A thousand false gods will stand together in the Pantheon; but if the ark of the true God enters Dagon's temple, Dagon must come down on his face and be dashed to pieces. Jehovah is God alone and will not brook a rival. Truth is of necessity intolerant of error." (Author unknown).

b. The results of the judgment of men about Christ are very MANY, but today they agree in this, that THEY CONTRADICT THE ONE AND ONLY TRUTH. Today some say, "He is a good man." But others say, "NO, but He deceives the people." Some say that He is divine, though not actually God. Others say that He has become God, though He was not always so. Others think Him a divine man. Some agree that his teachings were admirable for the occasions in which they were delivered, but that that they are somewhat stale in this advanced age. Others ridicule his teachings as altogether impractical.

c. The answers of the world are CONTRADICTORY; for, if Jesus was John the Baptist, He could not be Jeremiah. Certain spirits contradicted all the opinions which are registered in the text, for they called the master of the house Beelzebub. The apostles quoted to their Lord the best things that had been said of Him, but they hardly liked to foul their mouths with the baser titles.

d. The answers of the world recorded here are RESPECTFUL. "It is usual nowadays to speak very respectfully of Him…if there can be any respectfulness in words which deny His Godhead. Today, they tear the seamless garment of the crucified. They retain His example and profess to value it; but His sacrifice they fling aside as a rag of superstition." (Author unknown). They dare to deny His miracles while they applaud His precepts: they will have nothing to do with the doctrine of the cross; but with the self-denial of the cross they are enamored. Our lord will not be so divided. Those who do not take a whole Christ take none of Him at all.

e. The world's answers are EVERY ONE OF THEM WRONG. In the favorable summary given here, not one conjecture of men is correct. Jesus is not John the Baptist, or Elijah, or Jeremiah, or one of the prophets. Assuredly He is not Beelzebub. The people of that day did not know who Jesus was. The same is true of so many millions today. Evangelism answers that question accurately for them or it is not evangelism at all. Those of that day and those of this day do not know Him or His Father. The character of Jesus is much too hard a nut for the philosophic to crack.

f. The answers of the world are all UNBLESSED. Gazing at Jesus as John the Baptist, or Elijah, or Jeremiah brings no blessing with it. The only answer that brings blessing is the one Peter gave: "You are the Christ, the Son of the Living God." Peter could not know that answer without divine revelation (God opening his heart to believe). Neither can anyone today know that answer unless God opens their heart. Their heart is opened when they hear the message of the gospel in plain language. Jesus told Nicodemus that the spiritual can only be known by the power of the Spirit.

4. HOW DOES THE ANSWER THAT SIMON PETER GAVE DIFFER FROM THE ANSWERS OF THE WORLD?

a. It is more serious, more thoughtful, and more personal. People of the world didn't know how to answer that question then, and they don't know how to answer it now. Evangelism answers the question for them so that the Spirit may open their hearts to believe. Jesus is very disturbing. He divides among people.

b. The only appropriate answer is the one Simon Peter gave—an answer that came not from within him—an answer that, according to Jesus, was given to him by the Holy Spirit. The implication of the text is that Peter was only the spokesperson—that all the rest would have said the same thing. The important thing now is, WHO DO YOU SAY THAT HE IS? Who do you believe Him to be personally, and who do you tell others that He is?

c. The answer of the apostles was clearer, more definite, and more assured. It was a unanimous answer. That is the key point of our unity. We may differ on many things, but the answer of who Jesus is must have unity: He is the Christ, the Son of the Living God.

5. IS THE ANSWER PERMANENT?

a. This answer must also be permanent. Apostasy is going back on that answer. He is prophet, priest and king. He is the only Lord and Savior—the Way, the Truth, and the Life.

b. This is the one answer that GLORIFIES JESUS CHRIST, and He must receive all the glory. It is thus the answer that INFLUENCES others to come to Him. A watered down Christ attracts no one.

c. This answer does not come by reasoning but by revelation—revelation from the Holy Spirit—God opening the heart to believe. Our message is intended to give them the facts of the gospel, but only the Holy Spirit can make them understand. When He makes them understand, God opens their hearts, gives them faith to believe, and they are born again—the NEW BIRTH giving them eternal life from Him and with Him.

d. The New Birth gives a new nature—a nature that grows into purity and maturity in Him.

5. HOW ARE WE TO GIVE THIS ANSWER?

a. Not with formality or casualness. It must be given with

CERTAINTY OF HEART—heart-to-heart. It is good to read of Him in documents, and to hear of Him in lectures, but the only way to eternal life is for the Holy Spirit to reveal Jesus Christ to you. At the time the Holy Spirit reveals Christ to a person, He reveals the person to himself. Like Isaiah of old, we cannot stand in the presence of Jesus and not see ourselves as a sinner (I remember seeing a woman's white sheets hung on the line above the freshly fallen snow—there was no comparison of the white sheets to the freshly fallen snow—when I see myself up against Jesus, I get the same sensation). Seeing ourselves as a sinner causes us to repent and believe in Him as Lord and Savior. Seeing ourselves brings humiliation, contrition, repentance and renewal. We are moved to desire His holiness—to be like Jesus, and that brings salvation.

Once we come to that point, we have an inner rest and peace. We recognize that we are now at peace with God and with others and with self. This peace abides forever—we can never lose it.

There are privileges that accompany this new relationship: eternal life, the favor of God, children of God, and useful service to Him. As we are built up in Him, we desire to get others to be in Him and build them up in Him.

Walter Robbins was a young man I baptized. He had no formal education and little leadership ability. Yet, within the three months he lived after accepting Christ, he led forty-four people to accept Christ as Lord and Savior. Even at his funeral after his tragic death some were testifying of Christ's power in their lives—power they discovered because of Walter's testimony. He was a testimony of the power of the gospel in his own life, but also of the power through him to lead these many others to faith in Christ also.

SPIRITUAL GIFTS AND EVANGELISM

WHATEVER YOUR SPIRITUAL GIFT YOU CAN DO THE WORK OF EVANGELISM (Note: there is no spiritual gift of evangelism mentioned in the Bible; there is the gift of the evangelist to the church; there is the task of evangelism with whatever your spiritual gift may be). God has many laws—some related to spiritual things; some related to natural things. It is to one of His natural laws that I now turn to encourage you to do the work of evangelism—namely, the law of seed and harvest. This law is as immutable as the law of gravity. It cannot be broken; instead, you will be broken upon it. For example, if you jump off a tall building you will be broken when you fall, because of God's law of gravity.

> **LAW OF SEED AND HARVEST**
>
> Reap what you sow
>
> Reap in time
>
> Reap somewhere
>
> Reap in proportion
>
> Sowing and reaping are hard work

Just as surely as God's law of gravity holds, so does God's law of seed and harvest. Read about it in Galatians 6: 7-9: "Be not deceived; God is not mocked: for whatsoever a man sows, that shall he also reap. For he that sows to the flesh shall of the flesh reap corruption; but he that sows to the Spirit shall of the Spirit reap life everlasting. And let us not be weary in well doing: for in due season we shall reap, if we faint not." When you sow corn don't expect to reap wheat, or if you sow peas don't expect to reap turnips.

What you sow is what you reap. (See also Job 4: 8; Hosea 8: 7; 10: 12, 13; Jeremiah 4: 3; Proverbs 11: 18).

Some time ago I was in a certain place. There were thousands of beautiful trees, but I did not know what kind of trees they were. When I stopped and looked, there were almonds all over the ground under the trees, and almonds attached to the branches. I said, "Aha! Here we have a fig tree." That is ridiculous. They were almond trees—all of them.

You will reap in time. You may not reap immediately, but you will reap in time. You can grow turnips in a few weeks, but it takes years to grow an oak tree. However, the oak tree will last longer. You can sow to the flesh in a short time, and in an easy way, but it is hard work and takes time to

> *There is no gift of evangelism mentioned in the Bible, only the gift of the evangelist to the church.*
>
> *There is the task of evangelism for everyone with whatever spiritual gift(s) that person*

sow to the Spirit. Don't get discouraged though, for you will reap if you don't faint. There were many times I didn't see immediate results, but they came in God's time which was best. I can recall some that it was more than two dozen times that I presented to them the gospel before they came to Christ.

You may not reap where you sow, but you will reap somewhere. Note what Jesus said in John 4: 35-38: "Say not ye, there are yet four months, and then comes the harvest? Behold, I say unto you, lift up your eyes, and look on the fields; for they are white already to harvest. And he that reaps receives wages and gathers fruit unto life eternal; that both he that sows and he that reaps may rejoice together. And herein is that saying true, one sows, and another reaps. I sent you to reap that whereon you bestowed no labor: other men labored, and you are entered into their labors." At times I have reaped where others sowed; at other times, other people have reaped where I sowed ("I have planted, Apollos watered; but God gave the increase" 1 Corinthians 3: 6). The bottom line is that it doesn't matter who does the sowing or the reaping—just that God is glorified as people are born again.

You will reap in proportion to the amount you sow. Read 2 Corinthians 9: 6: "But I say, He which sows sparingly shall reap sparingly; and he which sows bountifully, shall reap bountifully." Much sowing, large harvest; little sowing, small harvest.

Sowing and reaping are hard work. You must brave unfavorable conditions to sow and reap. Sowing and reaping are also heart-rending work. Psalms 126: 5,6: "They that sow in tears shall reap in joy. He that goes forth and weeps, bearing precious seed, shall doubtless come again with rejoicing, bringing his sheaves with him." I have planted seed when the cold wind brought tears to my eyes. I have witnessed when it broke my heart over the condition of the person to whom I was witnessing. But I have enjoyed the harvest of the seeds I sowed in the cold, and I have rejoiced in the harvest of the souls that I shared the gospel with. Not only have I rejoiced, but God and His angels rejoiced with me (See Luke 15: 7, 10, 24). It is work to sow, but it brings joy when the harvest comes.

EVANGELISM IN THE POWER OF THE HOLY SPIRIT

I do a lot of work in my garden. I usually wear gloves when I do. But I have noticed that if I lay the gloves besides the shovel or hoe handles, nothing gets accomplished. I can command the gloves, yell at the gloves, criticize the gloves, and even get angry at the gloves, but until I put my hands (life) into the gloves they will never accomplish anything.

I have also noticed that if my hand is to fit into the glove that it must be empty of other objects. The same is true in my life: if the Holy Spirit is to fill me, I must be empty of self and sin.

It is the same with our labor in the Lord. We can do nothing good and lasting without the Holy Spirit ("Without Me you can do nothing"). We sometimes translate that as "you can't do much." But it is "nothing" that we accomplish without Him. In order to sow effectively and reap effectively we must be filled with the Holy Spirit. Until He, the Source of spiritual life, fills me I am useless.

How to be filled with the Holy Spirit

I will use an acrostic (CRAB) to describe being filled with the Holy Spirit.

C-onfess: 1 John 1: 9: "If we confess our sins, He is faithful and just to forgive our sins and to cleanse us from all unrighteousness." Every sin, large and small, must be confessed to God. "He that conceals his sins shall not prosper; but he that confesses and forsakes them will prosper" (paraphrase of Proverbs 28: 13). A right relationship cannot be restored until one confesses to God what He knows and you know to be true.

R-epent: "If I cherish sin in my heart, the Lord will not hear me." (Ps. 66: 18). "Testifying to Jews and Greeks alike, repentance toward God and faith in our Lord Jesus Christ" (Acts 20:21). Please note in Revelation the counsel of God to the churches to repent (It is the church members that need to repent). There must be a turning from sin that demonstrates our sincerity and faith. Too little emphasis is placed on repentance in modern-day preaching.

A-sk: "So I say to you, keep asking, and it will be given to you. Keep searching, and you will find. Keep knocking, and the door will be opened to you. For everyone who asks receives, and the one who searches finds, and to the one who knocks, the door will be opened. What father among you, if his son asks for a fish, will give him a snake instead of a fish? Or if he asks for an egg, will give him a scorpion? If you then, who are evil, know how to give good gifts to your children, how much more will the heavenly Father give the Holy Spirit to them who ask for Him?" (Luke 11: 9-13). All you need to do is to ask your Father and He will give the Holy Spirit. However, He only gives His Spirit for three reasons: praise, power, and service. He does not give Him for your self-glory.

B-elieve: No scripture reference is given here because inherent in all of God's Word and promises is the element of faith. Don't wait for a feeling or a sign. The Spirit will be there (He lives inside the believer) when you are in need of power, or when you start to praise or serve God. Martin Luther was once asked if he had dying grace. He replied that he didn't have it and wouldn't get it until it was time to die. The Spirit's power will show up when you are at the end of yours.

I once prayed sincerely for a group of people that I wanted to visit and present the gospel. As I visited God's Spirit was so present that 19 people came to faith in Christ that morning. I witnessed far beyond the lunch hour and felt no hunger ("I have food to eat that you don't know about"). On my way home, I thought about a twelve year old boy I wanted to witness to. I said to myself, "I am going by and win him to the Lord." He was very gracious and listened carefully to me as I spoke of the gospel to him, but when I asked him to pray and receive the Lord he would not. Suddenly, my heart was pierced as the Holy Spirit said to me, "You can present the gospel in human strength, but only I can open the heart to believe."

I apologized to the boy, confessing my sin, and asked him, along with the Holy Spirit to forgive me. Both did forgive. To my surprise, the boy said, "Now, I want to pray to receive Christ." "Without Me, you can do nothing."

FOUR AGENCIES TO CHRISTIAN MATURITY AND WITNESSING

> *Plowmen*
> *Sowers*
> *Reapers*
> *Treaders*

In bringing people to a full Christian life there are four steps. These steps may come rapidly, or they may come slowly. They may be done by one person or they may be done by many persons. They are found in Amos 9: 13: "Behold, the days come says the Lord, that the plowman shall overtake the reaper, and the treader of grapes him that sows seed; and the mountains shall drop sweet wine, and all the hills shall melt." (See also Isaiah 28: 23-29: These are prophecies concerning Israel, but I am taking them as a lesson for us in evangelism).

1 The first agents are the plowmen. These are the cultivators. They prepare the soil for the sowing of the seed. In the spiritual sense this is done by the kind of life one lives. People see a difference in us and want to know what it is. A bank teller who served me regularly one day asked why I was so happy and always smiling. She said, "I have watched you, and I want whatever it is that you have that makes you so happy." There was no line in the bank, so I shared the gospel with her and she prayed right there to receive Him as her Lord and Savior. Every Christian **CAN AND SHOULD CULTIVATE**.

However, wouldn't it be ludicrous to plow the ground every day of the year? That would either make a dust bowl or a mud hole. Wouldn't it be ridiculous for a person, on his death bed to say, "You know, Charlie Brown lived such a good life. I wonder what made the difference in him?"

2. The second agents are the <u>sowers</u> of the seeds. These are the ones who put the seed into the cultivated soil. In the spiritual sense these are the ones who scatter the Word of God (See Jesus' parables concerning the sower and the harvest: Luke 8: 4-15). They are called witnesses. A witness is one who tells what he has seen, heard or experienced. There is a sense in which some things one does gives a testimony (See cultivators above) (i.e. a kiss testifies of one's love to another, or baptism testifies of one's love for Christ), but in order to witness, one must open his mouth and tells what he has seen, heard or experienced. Suppose, for example, that you see an auto accident on your street. The police take a report, and later you are called to the court. When you are on the witness stand you are sworn to tell the whole truth and nothing but the truth. The attorney queries into whether you saw the accident in question. When it is affirmed that you saw the accident, you are asked to tell the court what you saw. However, you turn to the judge and say, "Your Honor, I am an honest person. I don't get drunk, I don't lie, I don't cheat. I pay my bills, go to church, am good to my neighbors, and work at an honest job. I think my life ought to be my witness." The judge would tell you to tell the court what you saw.

Now, if the defense attorney can prove you to be a person of bad character and reputation, your witness (testimony) would be thrown out of court because you were discredited. But your life is not your witness; it is only cultivation. Your life does not sow seed; it plows the ground. Could it be that you do not witness because you know that your testimony will be, or has been, discredited?

The Holy Spirit is God's attorney; you are His witness; the world around is the jury. Therefore, tell what you have seen, heard, or experienced. And live in such a way that your witness will not be discredited.

Again, wouldn't it be ridiculous for a person to never do any cultivating, and only sow seeds every day of the year? He must take time to prepare the ground or else he will waste the seed. The birds will get the seeds. By the same token, he cannot just plow and sow; he must also reap. He has at some point to put in the sickle and harvest (See Acts 1: 8; Revelation 1: 2; 1 John 1: 1-3).

3. That brings us to the third agent in bringing about Christian maturity—the reapers. This step is the harvest. In the spiritual sense the reapers are the disciple-winners (the soul-winners: since the Holy Spirit is the only soul-winner, I use the other phrase). These are the ones who actually "draw the net" by opening the Word of God, and leading people to confess their faith in Jesus Christ as Lord and Savior. If you really want to, you can progress to this joyful stage. Have you matured from a cultivator, to a witness, to a disciple-winner?

4. The fourth agent is the treader of grapes. This is the person, who after the harvest is gathered, sets about to do away with the dross and preserve the best of the harvest. This is discipleship at its best. The treader of the grapes tromps all over the grapes (discipline and exhortation) so that the best part of the grapes may be preserved. The hull and the pulp are thrown away. The juice is kept. The same thing must be done in relation to Christians. They must be squeezed in order to bring out the best. The pastors and teachers sometimes have to "tromp all over them" to bring out the juice and do away with the dross. This is painful for the treader, but it is for the good of the grape. It can also be painful to the grape, but it is necessary in order to produce the "peaceable fruit of righteousness."

The problem is not with the harvest; it is with the lack of harvesters.

Can you picture yourself involved in one or more of these processes? Can you imagine growing from one stage to another? The Holy Spirit is there to enable you to do so. Just ask Him to fill you, and volunteer for the Lord's army.

A HUMAN ANALOGY FOR AMOS 9: 13

The Lord is willing to take a person where he is and lead him to where he ought to be. He takes us through four stages.

We begin in the EGG stage. As the egg is warmed the seed is also. This is your stage of being a cultivator.

Next, is the LARVA stage. This would be handing out tracts; bringing people to gospel services and praying for them daily.

Third, is the CATERPILLAR stage. This would be telling others what God has done in your life with the hope they will be convinced that He can do the same for them.

The fourth is the BUTTERFLY stage. This would be actually taking your Bible and leading someone to receive Christ as their Lord and Savior. This is disciple-winning at its maturity.

We are tempted to not do any of these by Satan. It is important to remember two things when this happens: a) Witnessing is not easy. It is easier to preach to a crowd. b) There are many ways of witnessing for Christ (prayer, leaflet or tracts, letter writing, personal media, etc.), but you must go on to other things. You can talk about anything or everything else; you can talk about Christ.

INTENTIONAL EVANGELISM

```
INTENTIONAL EVANGELISM

Not confrontational
Not Generational
Not Accidental
Relational
Any kind better than none
```

Knowing therefore the terror of the Lord, we persuade men. (the Apostle Paul)

Acts 16: 14: A woman named Lydia, a dealer in purple cloth from the city of Thyatira, who worshipped God, was listening. The Lord opened her heart to pay attention to what was spoken by Paul."

In my earlier years I tried "confrontational evangelism." That is, I made it my goal to present the gospel to every person I could. I am sure that I offended many people by trying to make them listen to the gospel, whether they wanted to or not. I have come away from some encounters feeling that I have "thrown my pearls before swine, and they have turned and bitten me." As I have grown in the Lord and have come to understand more Scriptures (See the text), I have come to believe that "intentional evangelism" is better. That is, I intend to share the gospel with anyone that God will open the door for me to do so—I want to share with those whose heart God has opened. Since I don't know which hearts the Lord has opened, I am made entirely dependent upon the Holy Spirit to show me the ones to whom I am to witness. I have come to practice what I call "the theology of the white harvest."

Jesus told us that the problem is not with the harvest—He said, "The harvest is plentiful." The problem, according to Jesus, is with the harvesters, "but the workers are few; pray that the Lord of the harvest will thrust forth harvesters." All over the world God has people ready to hear the gospel, but He does not have intentional workers ready to share the gospel. I want to share with you my concepts on intentional evangelism.

First, I have already **contrasted it with confrontational evangelism**. God does not authorize us to "button-hole" people and force them to hear the gospel. Jesus told his disciples that if a place would not receive them, they should move on to another place, for they would not cover all the places before His return. There are so many who are ready to hear the gospel that we need not waste our time in senseless arguments with those whose minds are already made up. I once heard it said that the Holy Spirit is a gentleman— that He does not force Himself upon anyone. I believe that to be true. Therefore, if I mimic Him, I will also be a gentleman and not try to force myself or my ideas on someone who is unwilling to hear.

Second, I wish to **compare intentional evangelism with generational evangelism**. Many churches do a wonderful job of reaching the children that grow up among them. That is highly commendable, but, sad to say, many churches don't even do this. If a church preaches the gospel faithfully, and consistently invites people to profess Christ as Lord, they will be good at generational evangelism. However, if that church is to grow, it must go beyond generational evangelism and practice intentional evangelism— reaching out to those who are not in their church. After all, most of those kids will soon move away.

Third, I wish to point out that intentional evangelism is **the fruit of relational evangelism**. I totally agree that we need to build relationships with lost people in order to reach them. However, I don't think we will reach many of those with whom we build relationships unless we intentionally probe to find out if the Lord has opened their heart to the gospel. Any lost person is more likely to listen to a friend than to a total stranger who appears to be placing him in a corner. Intentional evangelism assures that we will watch under the guidance of the Holy Spirit to see if God has opened their hearts to hear the gospel. Once we sense their hearts are open, we intentionally share with them what we know about salvation and eternal life, inviting them to make a deliberate decision.

Finally, fourth, intentional evangelism is **preferred over accidental evangelism**. Really, I don't believe it is an accident when people come to Christ. I am only using this phrase to describe those moments when God is so involved in a person's life that He overwhelms us with the understanding that this person is ready to be saved. I once was preaching to a group of minimum security prisoners. I had not been speaking but about ten minutes when one of them said, "Alright! Already! When can I ask Jesus into my heart?" I stopped preaching and invited him along with any of the other of his colleagues to come to Christ. Dozens came and professed Jesus as Lord. I couldn't help but lead those men to Christ—in human terms I led them to Christ on an accident—in heavenly terms they came to Christ because God had orchestrated it.

Intentional evangelism is much preferred to NO EVANGELISM. I find that unless I keep before me the "terror of the Lord," and thereby share the gospel with as many as I sense God has opened their heart, I tend to do no evangelism. If I am not intentional in my desire and willingness to share the gospel, I find that I don't share it. In fact, I find times when I walk away from an encounter with another person and realize that they were ready to hear, but I was not ready to share.

Let me give you two illustrations of intentional evangelism. One, I was going in for outpatient surgery. I sat in the parking lot and prayed, "Lord, I intend to share the gospel if You will open the door for me to do so." When I got in for the surgery the person performing the surgery was a teaching surgeon. She had her whole class in to watch her perform surgery on my arm. The second question I was asked was, "How did you and your wife stay married so long?" Wow! The door was open, and for the next forty-five minutes while the surgeon was working on my arm, I stole her class and preached the gospel to them. Two, I swim with a person who has the same name as I do. I had been praying for an opportunity to share with him. As he came dog-paddling down the pool, he asked me, "Wayne, why do they call it Good Friday? It certainly was not good for Jesus." Once again, the door was open, and for the next 12 minutes I was able to share, not only with him, but also some others who were in the pool with us. Here's the point—if I had not been intentional, I might have not recognized the open hearts to hear the gospel.

TWELVE REASONS FOR INTENTIONAL EVANGELISM

We are sent
Fosters obedience
Imitates Jesus
Copies the Apostles
Shares our testimony
Sees people correctly
Protects us from indifference
Proves a Spirit-filled life
Uses spiritual gifts
Avoids excuses
Commended by Jesus
Avoids loss of rewards.

Next, I want to point out that the Triune God practices intentional evangelism. The Father intentionally sent the Son (John 3: 16-18). The Son intentionally died in our place ("No man takes My life from Me. I lay it down of my own accord"). The Holy Spirit intentionally opens people's hearts (John 16: 8-11).

Lastly, I will give you twelve reasons for intentional evangelism.

1. We are sent to do intentional evangelism (All four gospels give the Great Commission in varying forms, and the Book of Acts repeats it). Last words are important. Jesus' last words were that we are to take the gospel to the whole world. For 48 years I have honored the

last words of my earthly father. Should I not follow the last words of my heavenly Father?

2. It enables us to be obedient to the Father (See Matthew 28: 18-20; Mark 16: 14-15 & 19-20; Luke 24: 45-49; John 20: 19-23). The cited scripture references are the differing versions of the Great Commission. We need to remind ourselves what Samuel told Saul: "Then Samuel said: Does the Lord take pleasure in burnt offerings and sacrifices as much as in obeying the Lord? Look: to obey is better than sacrifices, to pay attention is better than the fat of rams. For rebellion is like the sin of divination, and defiance is like wickedness and idolatry. Because you have rejected the word of the Lord, He has rejected you as king." (1 Sam. 15: 22-23).

3. It empowers us to imitate Jesus (Study His life and note all the times He intentionally shared the good news). Look, for example at John 4 concerning the Woman of Sychar. I find some interesting principles in His lifestyle. First, He had a burden for the needs of lost people (v. 4). The Scripture said that He had a moral obligation to go through Samaria so He could have this encounter (The Greek word *dei* indicates this). Second, He witnessed to her even though He was tired (v. 6). As one studies the Scriptures, he will find Jesus going the second mile in personal encounters. Third, He did not minimize the importance of a single interview. In fact, leading the woman to faith resulted in the whole city hearing the gospel and many of them turning to Christ. Fourth, He loved her. She sensed it and was receptive to His words because of that sense of love for her. Fifth, He asked a favor from her (v. 7). It is effective to ask a question or a favor from those with whom we share. The old saying, "People don't care how much we know until they know how much we care," is accurate. Sixth, He started the conversation where she was. She needed water and He talked about thirsts—eternal thirsts. While we are working, God is working. Seventh, He had no class distinction. She was totally surprised that He a Jewish man would have interest in her a Samaritan woman. People of that day just didn't do that. Eighth, He offered her satisfaction (vv. 13, 14). The

Scriptures says that God has put eternity in the heart of every person…that everyone without Christ has an emptiness that only God can fill. We are not out to prove how bad people are, but to prove how good God is. Jesus dealt with her with love and truth.

We must balance love and truth. Love without truth is sentimentalism. Truth without love is legalism. He showed that He loved her, but He also confronted her with her immoral life-style.

Ninth, He aroused curiosity (v. 15), causing deep interest in what He had to say. Tenth, He didn't get sidetracked when she wanted to argue about denominations (vv. 19-24). He didn't argue; He brought her to her real need. Eleventh, He pointed out that sin must be dealt with (v. 16). If there is no recognition of sin, there is no sense of repentance. Repentance and faith are the opposite sides of the coin (Testifying to Jews and Greeks alike, repentance toward God and faith in our Lord Jesus Christ). Twelfth, He staked His witness on the Scriptures (v. 22). "Salvation is of the Jews" is a quote from the Old Testament which was the only Scripture she knew. Thirteenth, He urged upon her the importance of making a decision for Him at that time (Behold, today is the day of salvation; behold, now is the accepted time).

Summarizing Jesus' example I note these general statements. One, we must believe that every individual is worth saving. Two, we must find a common object for interest as a contact point. Three, we must let people know that we love them and are interested in them. Four, we must bring them face to face with the fact of their sin and the answer to their sin, Jesus. Five, we must avoid heated arguments. In another place I have cautioned about winning an argument but losing a soul. Six, we must make Christ's claim on their life immediate. Now is the time. Draw the net while the fish is in the net. Reel in the line while the fish is on the hook.

4. It encourages us to copy the apostles (See Acts 3: 1-19 where Peter and John shared intentionally; Acts 10: 34-43 where Peter intentionally broke racial barriers to share the gospel; Romans 15:

18-21 where Paul described his plan of intentional evangelism).

5. It permits us to share our testimony (Acts 20: 21): People will argue with the Bible but will not argue with your personal testimony. Paul speaks of testifying about his experience. At Pentecost Peter used many other words of testimony in sharing the gospel with the crowd.

6.It protects us from indifference (See 2 Timothy 1: 6-7 where Paul reminds Timothy of the responsibility for all of us to intentionally share the good news). We always tend toward coolness. This requires that we stoke the coals, fan the flame, and put fuel on the fire.

8. It helps us to see people correctly (Not as a source of self-gratification, but as a person for whom Jesus died—not as an object of scorn, but of divine pity: Matthew 9: 35-38).

8. It proves we are filled with the Holy Spirit (See Acts 1: 8). The fact is, that if we are filled with the Holy Spirit, we will be witnesses. No witness, no filling.

9. It facilitates the use of our spiritual gifts (See Matthew 25: 14-30—whatever gift we have is to be used in obedience to the Great Commission and the Great Commandment).

10. It helps us avoid excuses (See Luke 14: 15-24). The three excuses in this passage are: I have something more important to do; I have some place more important to go; and, I have someone more important to see. What thing is more important than obedience to Christ? What place is more important that where Christ sent us? What person is more important to please than Christ?

11. It receives the commendation of Jesus Christ (See Matthew 25: 21 & 23). The commendation is one of joy in the Lord's heart that we have obeyed, and one of joy in our hearts that we will enter into the joy of our Lord and be given a place of responsibility in His eternal kingdom.

12. It avoids the loss of rewards (Matthew 25: 28-30 & 1 Corinthians

3: 5-15). It is clear that the judgment of our sins was dealt with at the cross, and we will never face that judgment. It is also clear that we will be judged as to our rewards. Don't you want to have some trophies to place at the feet of Jesus when you get to heaven?

There are many methods of sharing the good news. One is not necessarily better than the other. Find one that you are comfortable with and intentionally tell the good news to anyone that you feel the Lord has opened his heart. Don't criticize my method. I will not criticize your method, unless your method is to avoid your responsibility. There is no spiritual gift of evangelism. There is a spiritual gift of the evangelist. There is the responsibility of every born again believer to share his faith with those whose hearts the Lord opens. In fact, we are to share the good news and leave the results in the hands of God.

THE GOSPEL INVITATION

As I write on this subject, I do not wish to hold myself as the authority, nor do I wish to be a know-it-all. However, if experience is the best teacher, then I have a solid education on evangelistic invitations. My education in calling people to Christ has taken me the space of 66 years of public and private gospel ministry along with preaching the gospel on almost all of the continents of the world. I have preached the gospel in all kinds of places, under all manner of circumstances, and with both ease and hardships. I have read every work I can find on this subject. I have studied the great evangelists.

These principles have been used to train hundreds of evangelists as I worked in cooperation with the Evangelism Division of the North American Mission Board, as well as adjunct professor of evangelism at California Baptist University. One of the most gratifying reports I have received in my ministry was when a pastor told me that he perused the leading churches in baptisms in California, and that 19 of the top 25 churches had pastors who had been in my classes at CBU.

I confess to being an avid reader with an ability to retain much of what I read. As a result, things are expressed in this volume that I have read without being able to recall where I read them. There is no attempt to give proper credits in this volume except to quote the person who said it, completely ignoring a bibliography. I am not intentionally guilty of plagiarism. I am guilty of wanting to expand the kingdom of God.

God has used these methods in every area of this world where our teams have ministered, and we have seen more than one-half million (500,000) people responding positively to the call of our Lord through the simple presentation of the simple facts of the gospel of Jesus Christ. I want God to have all the glory. Everything I am and all that I have is a direct gift from Him. Praise His holy name—all that is within me, praise His holy name.

The purpose of my writing is that we may reach as many as we can, as rapidly as we can, for the glory of the One who called us and saved us. There is no desire for credit in this world. Our credit will come at the Bema Judgment seat of our Lord when we hear Him say, "Well done, good and faithful servants. You have been faithful...enter into the joy of your Lord."

As with many other works, the plans in this volume will do you no good unless you work the plans. Revival comes through prayer and preaching. Here is the gist of a message that I preached on prayer and preaching for revival:

Title: **Revival Through Prayer and Preaching**; Text: Habakkuk 3: 2: Lord, I have heard a report about YOU: Lord, I stand in awe of Your deeds. Revive Your work in these years; make it known in these years. In Your wrath remember mercy? Romans 1: 16-17: For I am not ashamed of the gospel, because it is God's power for salvation to everyone who believes, first to the Jew, and also to the Greek. For in it God's righteousness is revealed from faith to faith, just as it is written: **The righteous will live by faith**.

Proposition: The Church of today is involved in forms of idolatry (some with inanimate icons; others with living icons such as sports idols, etc). She is careless, forgetful of God, and involved in many evil practices. We need to call the Church back to God by praying along with Habakkuk for revival and preaching along with Paul without any shame the real gospel of Jesus Christ.

Objective: To call the church back to prayer and preaching, seeking God's face in revival.

Introduction: Nahum had comforted Judah with the assurance that the power of Assyria should be overthrown, though for a time it was permitted to afflict the people of God. Habakkuk warns Judah of another great empire which was commissioned by Jehovah to chastise her backslidings. There had been a partial reformation under Josiah, but it had not gone far enough. The coming of Babylon would bring devastation and captivity. Judah felt that because Nineveh had fallen, she was safe, but they underestimated the menace of Babylon. Habakkuk is commissioned to warn them, that in spite of them being cured of idolatry and selfish luxury, concerning their carelessness, forgetfulness of God, and vicious evil practices, there was danger directly in their path.

Some years ago, I preached at an evangelism conference in Redding, CA. There was a young pastor in attendance that was visibly shaken and angry at me, the messenger. He later told me that he actually looked for me in the parking lot, because he wanted to physically beat me up. But as he went away, the Holy Spirit convicted him to the extent that he began to take the advice that I had given in the message. He went back and led his church to prayer and the preaching of the gospel. His ministry was revolutionized, and his church exploded with growth, because they went back to prayer and the preaching of the gospel.

Now, I am certain that some of you will become angry with me over this message. I also fear that some of you will think I am self-serving by my thoughts. My prayer is that the Holy Spirit will affect in you what He did in that young man long ago, and that your ministry will be revitalized, and your church will begin to experience exponential growth.

First, I must deal with four major UNBIBLICAL MYTHS concerning ministry in this modern age. One myth says that **revivals no longer work**. We have been led to believe that we can no longer get people to attend concentrated days of meetings. That myth is denying a major biblical principle of revival that God put in place for the Jews. He gave them seven festivals that would insure that they met together and renewed fellowship and a spirit of unity that resulted in strengthening the nation. These seven feasts celebrated a different aspect of the life, death and resurrection of Jesus Christ (The Feast of Passover reminds us of redemption from sin. It was the time when Jesus Christ was offered as an atoning sacrifice for our sins. The Feast of Unleavened Bread followed immediately and reminds us of the importance of ridding ourselves of evil in our lives. The Feast of Firstfruits acknowledges that our deliverance comes from God alone through Jesus Christ. The Feast of Weeks (Pentecost, meaning 50) reminds us that we are to be grateful to God for all He has provided for us—it guarantees that our future resurrection is secure. The Feast of Trumpets reminds us of the Second Coming of Jesus Christ to rapture His bride, the Church. The Feast of Atonement reminds us that after the Church is raptured, God will turn His attention to Israel, and "all Israel will be saved." The Feast of Booths reminds that Christ will reign on the earth at a future time—a time when all believers from all nations will reign with Christ forever.

God put these feasts in place so that Israel would remain in a state of revival. Please notice that all of these feasts took major preparation and hard work. While I am not advocating that we celebrate the Jewish festivals, I want to remind us that revivals still work if we work them. You cannot just announce a meeting and expect people to come—you have to take steps that plan for them to come. Let's go back to God's pattern and plan for meetings that we pray break out into revival.

A second myth is that **visitation no longer works**—that we cannot visit people anymore. If God knew that there would come a time when visitation would not work, why didn't He leave out of the Bible the statements: "Go out into the highways and hedges and bring them (the down-and-outs) in;" Go out into the streets and lanes of the city and bring them (the up-and-outs) in? We just had a special meeting in our church with our two congregations (English-speaking and Spanish-speaking). We had 12 guests, with people saved from both groups, but they were all invited by door-to-door visitation by the Spanish youth. At any given time, you can make ten calls and God will have someone prepared to receive you.

A third myth is that the **vocational evangelist is no longer needed**. If that is true, why did God list them among the "gifts to the church" in Ephesians 4? Work up a plan to have a vocational evangelist in your church; work your plan; pray for God's blessing; have the meeting and watch God use His appointed methods. These evangelists are especially gifted in "drawing the net" with clarity, compassion and conviction. Don't give up on God's ways, regardless of what others may tell you. It will be hard work and careful preparation, especially the preparation of weeks of intentional prayer and visitation. Publicity helps to draw the crowd, but only the Holy Spirit can draw the individual to the cross of Jesus Christ.

A fourth myth is that **invitations no longer work**. They only work if you offer them. Why preach if you are not going to offer people an opportunity to respond. Perhaps, my writing on the invitation will encourage and instruct you on the invitation.

How can we recognize the NEED FOR REVIVAL? As in Habakkuk's case it will be manifested by a FEAR of God. "Though he was a pious man and a prophet, he was at the same time a philanthropist and a patriot, who could not contemplate without a shudder the decimation of his people or the desolation of his country; and neither can the Christian anticipate without apprehension those chastisements that are promised to himself or correction of his backslidings, and to the Church for her recovery from doctrinal aberration or spiritual declension." (*Pulpit Commentary*).

I am not speaking of a shrinking fear of God, but of a convictional fear of God, such as Adam and Eve had when they had sinned in the Garden of Eden. This fear comes from thoughts of His mighty Presence (Therefore I am terrified in His presence; when I consider this, I am afraid of Him. God has made my heart faint; the Almighty has terrified me" Job 23: 15-16). It also comes through the manifestation of His power (Those who live far away are awed by Your signs; You make east and west shout for joy' Palms. 65: 8) Again, this fear comes through the contemplation of His judgments ("I tremble in awe of You; I fear Your judgments" (Psalms 119: 120). IT MAY BE BETTER TO FALL INTO THE MERCIFUL HANDS OF GOD THAN TO FALL INTO THE HANDS OF THE ENEMY, BUT IT IS STILL A FEARFUL THING TO FALL INTO THE HANDS OF THE LIVING GOD. Hiding from God is the practice of sinners; hiding in God is the comfort of saints.

The CURE FOR THIS FEAR IS PRAYER AND PREACHING LEADING TO REVIVAL. We may pray for three specific things:

1) an acceleration of God working among us: "O Lord! Revive Your work in the midst of these years." His work is the deliverance of individuals and the Church collectively through afflictions and trials, as well as the overthrow of Satan from the legal and spiritual bondage of sin.

(2) The manifestation of His glory. "Make it known in these years." We need to experience, as churches, what Israel manifested when God was among them (a fear of the Jews fell upon the nations because of what God was doing among His people).

(3) A dispensation of His judgments. Habakkuk's prayer was not based on merit. He knew full well that what he asked could not be granted on the score of justice. It is the mercy of God that we need in these years.

(4) Habakkuk's prayer was based in an intelligent understanding of the sinful state they were in. Until we understand our backsliding, our prayers are not intelligent. His prayer was based in a full recognition of the connection of the ineffectiveness of the church and the moral degeneracy of the same church. Repentance is necessary. Again his prayer was based toward spiritual results above numerical or monetary results. The saving of souls is more important than the social life of the church. Finally, his prayer was impatient of any delay in its answer. He wanted a present blessing.

He did not want to spend one more night with the frogs (See Pharaoh). He wanted revival and he wanted it now.

What in addition to prayer brings revival? PREACHING THE GOSPEL. That is what Paul had in mind when the Holy Spirit led him to write that he was not ashamed of the gospel. The HCSB Study Bible asks and answers a question: "Why might someone be ashamed of the gospel? On the surface, the gospel seems like a very strange message. It is about a Jewish carpenter and teacher who was put to death on a cross by Pontius Pilate, Roman Governor of Judea in A.D. 26-36. The message says that this man Jesus was raised from the dead and is now Lord—the *kurios*. This title was used of God in the Greek Bible and was applied to the emperor by some Romans. Paul himself wrote that this message seemed foolish to Gentiles (1 Corinthians 1: 23) and was a stumbling block to Jews. A crucified Messiah seemed to be a contradiction in terms to the Jews. A crucified Jew seemed like foolishness to the Romans, who despised Jews in general...Paul had no confidence in his rhetorical skills to overcome the human objections to the message, but he knew the power of the Spirit to change the lives of people as they heard the good news about Jesus' death and resurrection." He felt that the gospel could change any person regardless of circumstances or magnitude of evil in their life.

Paul acknowledged that people are saved by faith, but that faith is not the cause of salvation. Instead, the cause of salvation is the grace of God (Ephesians 2; 8-9), the will of God (2 Peter 3: 9), and the Holy Spirit working in the life of the person (John 16: 5-11).

God's righteousness has three meanings: God always does what is right; God's actions are therefore always right; and, God's righteousness is a gift to all who place their faith in Jesus Christ as Lord and Savior. God's righteousness comes to us through faith from start to finish.

If we will go back to biblical methods and work in cooperation with the Holy Spirit, we will see revival come. God uses three agents in His revival plan: the Word of God (we must preach the Bible), the Spirit of God (we must preach the Bible in the power of the Holy Spirit), and, the Man of God (God limits Himself to using a person to preach the gospel in the power of the Holy Spirit.)

If you really want to learn how to be effective in calling people to Christ, three recommendations come to the front:

1. **Practice** by being faithful as a personal evangelist (the best way to learn how to give a public invitation is to lean to give a private one).

2. **Give** the public invitation the same way you give the private one (never ya'll come, but you come).

3. **Preach** a series of sermons based on one or more of the appeals that are listed for your consideration. As you practice, like a golf-swing, the skill of calling people to Christ will become ingrained in your mind and soul. Weave one of the methods into each sermon you preach, planning your invitation before you write your sermon. As you use these principles over time, they will become second nature to you. As a result, you will one day become aware that you are improving in the area of "drawing the net," "closing the deal," and getting people "to step across the line" for Jesus Christ.

A Quandary of preachers answered

I have heard many preachers say something like the following: I know how to build a good church and grow a congregation. But I feel totally inadequate when it comes to inviting people to make a decision for Christ." Statements like this are common to pastors around the world. It is an honest heart-cry that most pastors understand.

Others may say something like this: "I have been trained in the presentation of the gospel. I know several plans of presenting the gospel. I just don't seem to be able to bring the person from an understanding of the gospel facts to a commitment to the Christ of the gospel." These statements are very familiar as well. Having trained literally thousands of people in personal evangelism, I know the pain of this honest confession. I confess that I still struggle with this aspect of the work of calling people to Christ.

Why do we have this common problem? It seems that Satan attacks us at this point more than any other. He doesn't mind that people know the Bible. He doesn't even mind if they know the facts of the gospel. What he hates is that they know the Lord of the gospel. Therefore, he will do anything (intimidation, terrorization, or slander) to prevent us from drawing the net to pull in the fish. He doesn't care that we entice the fish; he just doesn't want us to land them.

I present this section with the hope that it will help you to be better at fishing for people, a more accomplished harvester of souls, and a more confident inviter of people to the Savior. Learn these principles and you will have the courage to "throw your nets on the other side of the boat." Practice these methods and you will find your nets breaking while you call for help from fellow fishermen. Put these into practice and you "will pull down your old barns (church buildings) and build larger ones." Include these ideas into your preaching and you will be much more effective at inviting people to trust your Lord as their Lord.

How To Give A Powerful Evangelistic Invitation?

As I have already mentioned, I have observed many great preachers who can skillfully answer the first three questions referred to in the preface of this work. However, I have noted there are few who can answer the fourth question adequately. The fourth question from my preface (How can I get it?) is all about the invitation.

Invitations are as old as Christianity. They just vary in methodology. I generally ask preachers a simple question: Why preach if you are not going to give an invitation? Over the years I have learned a couplet that has helped me greatly in the matter of giving an evangelistic invitation:

Impression Without Expression Leads to Suppression Which Results in Depression.

What is the use of impressing people with the truths of the gospel unless you are going to give them an opportunity to express their response to what they have been impressed with—what they have heard? As you will discover, in the following pages there are many kinds of invitations, and many ways to give them.

R. Alan Street wrote: "The first-century gospel preacher always concluded his evangelistic sermon with an appeal for the unconverted present to repent of their sins and place their faith in the crucified and resurrected Lord of glory. Often these appeals called upon the individuals additionally to demonstrate their sincerity by taking a public stand for Christ before friends, neighbors, and even enemies. This call for the sinner or new convert to make an initial public profession of faith is the basis for the modern-day practice of extending a public invitation. Two types of public invitation were used in New Testament times. The first called for sinners to demonstrate publicly their desire to repent and believe, then was used as a means of bringing them to a state of conversion. The second called upon new converts, who had been supernaturally transformed by the message, to witness to their new-found faith."

Adam and Eve were called out into an open confession before God. Moses called upon Israel to openly repent and believe. Joshua called for a public profession. Elijah called for a public demonstration of repentance and faith. Josiah called for public admission of guilt and a promise to change. Ezra demanded a public confession, as did Nehemiah. Jesus called publicly always. Can we do less?

The Best Way to Learn To Give A Good Public Invitation Is to Become Skilled in Giving A Personal Private Invitation. The Public Invitation is to Be the Same as the Private Invitation.

Cats and dogs are born in litters, but people come into the kingdom of God one by one. Become good at inviting people personally and you will become good at inviting them publicly. There is no such thing as mass evangelism. There is mass communication of the gospel, but the invitation is always personal and private.

As we know it, the "come forward" invitation was lost for many years, and in the eyes of some (See Martin Llyod-Jones, etal.) is a comparatively modern thing, though there have been some types of invitation to all preaching. I am under the opinion that the public "come forward" invitation was popularized, if not restarted, by Charles G. Finney. Critics of the "come forward" invitation claim that we cannot pin down exactly when the invitation, as we know it, began. That is not true (See the preceding paragraph quoting Dr. Streett: If you really desire to trace the history of the public invitation, read Dr. Streett's book: *The Effective Invitation*).

Why Billy Graham Was So Successful

Divine calling
Divine message
Divine arsenal
Divine enablement

On the other hand, many will say the invitation is the most important part of the gospel service. In fact, I recommend that one write his conclusion and his invitation appeal before he writes the rest of his sermon. It will help him stay on target as he writes his message.

Dr. Streett claims that there are four reasons why Billy Graham's invitations were so effective: a divine calling, a divine message, a divine arsenal, and a divine enablement. I believe that God still calls some to be evangelists (See also why Dr. Dan Nelson concluded that George Whitefield was so successful: confidence in the Word of God; a zeal for souls; and, animated, dynamic preaching: page 14, *A Burning and Shining Light*). . I contend that the message of the gospel is the power of God unto salvation. I believe that we need not feel it is our responsibility to draw people to Christ, but only preach the gospel in the power of the Holy Spirit—it is God's to call them. I also believe that God especially anoints the evangelists that he calls—anoints them in such a way that they are used to enable faith in those to whom they appeal. Billy Graham said, "Yes. It is a part of the gift of the evangelist." I also believe that everyone, whether called as an evangelist or not, can issue an invitation to sinners to come to Christ and expect positive results.

The New Testament pattern of the invitation was to lead people to respond positively by being baptized. It was unthinkable that one would profess Christ as Lord without being baptized. Hence, we see the Ethiopian Eunuch asking what hindered him from being baptized. Some will argue that the thief on the cross was not baptized. If the argument has to do with being baptized in order to be saved, the point is moot. If we are thinking of pleasing and obeying the Lord then one has to be baptized. Rest assured, though the thief was saved without baptism, could he have gotten off the cross, God would have demanded him to be baptized. Jesus always called people publicly; therefore, a public response is absolutely necessary. We are responsible to make sure people have the opportunity to profess faith in Him publicly.

Six Kinds of Gospel Invitations to the Lost

By kinds of invitations I mean the categories to whom the invitation is given. There are six basic types of invitation to those who are lost and four basic types to the Christians.

1. There is the invitation to those who are lost to **accept Jesus as Lord and Savior**. In our terminology a lost person is one who has never openly acknowledged that Jesus is Lord. Perhaps you will want to study the origin of the use of the word "lost" to describe people who are far away from God. You will find that study in the Gospel of Luke, chapter 15. There you will read about the lost sheep that got lost following its physical appetites; the lost coin that got lost by doing what comes naturally (round, it rolled; heavy, it fell; dead, it lay), losing its worth, and experiencing its inability to get back into the treasury; the lost younger son who got lost because of his rebellious actions; and the lost older son who got lost because of

his attitudes. So, when we call a person who is far away from God "lost" we are using the language of our Master, Jesus Christ.

There is the primary invitation to the lost to ask them to accept Christ as Lord and Savior, and to ask them to demonstrate their acceptance of Him by some sort of public profession (namely, walking down the aisle of the church, signing a commitment card, raising a hand, looking at the messenger, or being baptized).

Six Invitations to Lost People

Accept Christ as Lord and Savior

Public profession and baptism

Raise their hands if interested in becoming a Christian

A desire for prayer

To have someone visit them

Go home and think it over

We should never be ashamed of this invitation, because the gospel "is the power of God unto salvation to everyone who believes." We should never be intimidated because of the criticism of other people ("If I seek to please men, I am not the servant of Jesus Christ"). Considering that the highest time of receptivity to change occurs at the crucial points in life (funerals, surgeries, weddings, new home, new job, new child, etc.), I feel that I should invite people to Christ then ("strike while the iron is hot," "make hay when the sun is shining," "draw the net while the fish is in the net," "reel in the line while the fish is on the hook,"). A study of the use of the word "come" in the New Testament will convince anyone that we catch the spirit of our Lord Jesus and the spirit of the early church when we ask people to "come and make a decision for Christ." (Study the word "come" in passages like Matthew 10: 38; 11: 28-30; 16: 24; 22: 3; Luke 14: 17; John 5: 40; 6: 35; 2 Corinthians 6: 17; Hebrews 4:

16; and Revelation 22: 17). There are also other words like "follow," "confess," and "take up one's cross." When we ask people to come and make a decision for Christ, we follow the example of our Lord and His apostles.

2. The second invitation to the lost is to those who have believed in their heart but have never surrendered to a **public profession of faith and to baptism**—to confess with their mouth what they have believed in their heart. It is extremely important that each person who believes in his heart also confesses with his mouth (Matthew 10: 32, 33; Romans 10: 9, 10). It is also important that they declare their faith in Christ and their desire to be a part of His church through baptism (Matthew 3:12-17; 28: 18-20; Acts 2: 38; 8: 36-39, etc.). We all need benchmarks in our lives (a wedding ceremony to remind us that we are married, a graduation to remind us that we have completed the work, etc.) Public profession and baptism give one a benchmark to which he can go when Satan tempts him with unbelief.

3. Another invitation to the lost is to ask them to **raise their hands** if they are interested in becoming a Christian. With many people steps to a decision are necessary. I advocate progressive invitations only if they are open and honest. I feel it is wrong to "trap" people into something they don't want to do. For example, I feel it would be wrong to ask a person to raise his hand if he were interested, and, then, when he has raised his hand, say, "Alright, all of you who raised your hands, I want you to come on down to the front." I think it would be more honest to say, "By raising your hand you've indicated an interest in becoming a Christian. You've taken a brave step in the right direction. Now, why not go all the way and make that decision public by coming forward." This gives them an opportunity to either make the decision publicly or graciously, and without embarrassment to themselves or to others, to let you know they won't make the public profession right then. I feel this leaves the door open for future witnessing, while the former method may close the door for future opportunities of sharing the gospel again.

If someone comes to make a public decision because he was either trapped or shamed into it, there may be irreparable harm done. Or, if because he feels trapped or shamed, he turns away, distrust of Christians may turn him away completely. Jesus always gave a person the privilege of saying "yes" or "no." He used no tricks.

4. A fourth invitation to the lost is to ask them to give some kind of indication of a **desire for prayer**. They may indicate this desire by a raised hand, a look at the preacher, standing to their feet, etc. Again, openness and honesty are paramount if we would follow the New Testament example. I know some evangelists who use progressive invitations starting with the request that people raise their hands for prayer. It goes something like this: "Now, all of you who would like for me to pray for you raise your hand; next, all of you who raised your hands, I want you to come down to the front so I can pray for you…now, all of you who came down to the front, I want you to go to the counselling room."

I do not question the sincerity, or the integrity of those who use this method. I am also open to listen to anything or anyone that will help me reach more people for Christ. However, I am interested in reaching them for Christ, not just getting a public decision—not just get a name on a decision card. I feel it is much better, after having asked people to raise their hands for prayer, to pray for them right where they are. Then after prayer for them, it is perfectly honest to then say something like, "Now that I've prayed for you, why don't you come right out in the open for Christ? As an indication that you will, please come forward so we may rejoice with you in the decision you have made to follow Christ?"

My conviction is that we are sent to invite people to make Jesus their Lord…not to intimidate them into making a decision. In the long haul, this will reach more people for Christ. After all, do we depend upon our persuasiveness, or do we depend upon the Holy Spirit's drawing power to get men to Christ?

5. A fifth invitation to the lost is to ask them to indicate their desire to

have a visit from someone to further explain to them the implications of following Christ. The form of that invitation may be a raised hand, a signed card (this is preferable because it gives the proper contact information), a word to someone after the service, etc. Before giving this invitation, be sure of several things…that you know where to find them; that you are purposed to pray for them and to find them; and that you are determined to visit them. Tremendous damage could result if you do not follow through on this invitation.

6. A sixth invitation to the lost is to **go home and think about the decision**. This should be a last resort…do this only after every other invitation has been exhausted. On a night in Chicago many years ago, D. L. Moody preached a powerful message to a large audience. When he concluded his message, he asked the people to go home and think it over. That same night Mrs. O'Leary's cow kicked over the kerosene lantern that started a conflagration of a fire that was not quenched until it destroyed much of Chicago. Thousands of people were killed. It was then that Mr. Moody vowed that he would never preach again without asking people to commit themselves to Christ.

Four Kinds of Invitations to the Believer

To me a believer or Christian is one who has openly acknowledged Christ as Lord, and who participates in the Lord's work. All of us need to make open decisions for Christ from time to time.

1. The first invitation to the Christian that I list is an invitation for **rededication**. This invitation is necessary because carnality creeps in upon all of us. When we first surrender to Christ as Lord and Savior, we surrender all of ourselves to Him to the best of our knowledge, and we're zealous, "a house afire", as it were. But as we continue in the Christian walk, we tend to drift away ("lest we let these things slip"), or to take back territory that we once surrendered to Christ, and the zealous fire burns down to smoldering ashes ("He will not crush a bruised reed or extinguish a smoldering flame").

Therefore, we need to challenge folks to recommit (rededicate) their whole being— "to stir up" (2 Timothy 1: 6)—that fire for our Lord. Many times, this decision will be more life-changing as to outward life-style than when one first was saved. This is not an invitation that everyone in the church will respond to at one time. Yet, most likely, everyone in the church should respond to it as some time. As V. L. Stanfield said, "This should be the most accepted invitation in the church."

Four Invitations to Believers

Rededicate their life-renew commitment

Transfer membership

Exercise their spiritual gift(s) in service

Personal commitment to pray, witness, enlist others, accept a position of service, or to give finances

---

2. The second invitation to the Christian is to **transfer membership** from one church to another (a disclaimer: many churches no longer carefully guard a membership role, though it is required in order to have a 501C-3 tax-exempt organization). This is done in different ways in different churches. Some churches require a letter of commendation from the previous church. This is known as "transfer of membership by letter" (today, it would be more appropriate to say, "transfer by e-mail, etc.). In most cases where a letter of commendation cannot be received, or is not desired, one may join another church by a "statement of faith in Christ and his baptism into the body of Christ." This is known as "transfer of membership by statement." In some churches a person wishing to transfer membership from another church must be baptized into that church unless his previous church membership was in a group that held the same beliefs (a church of like faith and order) as the church he

wishes to join. In other churches all that is necessary is to express one's desire to join. There are some churches that carry no membership rolls, and those who attend (and only those who attend) faithfully make up the membership. The mobility of our society makes this an important invitation. Far too many move to another place and never become active in a church where they live. The kingdom of God suffers great loss because of this...loss in workers, talent, and money, etc.

3. The third invitation to the Christian is to **exercise their spiritual gift of service**. We are to call out "the called" to vocational service. Note, I didn't say "full-time" Christian service. I said "vocational" Christian service. Every Christian ought to be full-time in service to our Lord. Many people refer to me as a "full-time evangelist." I call myself a "vocational evangelist." Everyone is to be a full-time evangelist, but not many should be vocational evangelists. Therefore, we are to invite people to openly commit themselves to vocational Christian service.

There are several responsibilities of the Christian church related to this invitation. One, we are to pray that God will set apart these people for the work He has called them to do. "Therefore," said he (Jesus) unto them, "the harvest is truly great, but the laborers are few: pray ye therefore the Lord of the harvest, that he would send forth laborers into his harvest" (Luke10: 2). From my own experience of many years as a pastor and evangelist I know that God will answer this prayer. I have seen scores go out as a result of the prayers of God's people, and the challenge of the pastor or evangelist.

Two we are to call out those that show evidence of having a gift of vocational Christian service. With some the gift is evident immediately, while in others it takes time to see it. For years our policy has been to wait for the person to surrender to a ministry. But the New Testament pattern was quite different. It took the initiative to "set apart" those in whom they saw the gift. "As they ministered to the Lord, and fasted, the Holy Ghost, said, 'Separate me Barnabas and Saul for the work whereunto I have called them. And when they had fasted and prayed and laid their hands on them, they sent them away" (Acts 13: 2, 3). I recognize that, even after we call the gift to their attention, they must surrender to God in response to His call. So, whether we say, "surrender to vocational Christian service," or "request that they exercise their spiritual gift of vocational Christian service," this invitation is still valid, and needs to be given.

Three, we are responsible to support those who respond to God's call. We are to support them by our prayers..." Brothers, pray for us" (1 Thessalonians 5: 25); "Peter therefore was kept in prison: but prayer was made without ceasing of the church unto God for him" (Acts 12: 5). We are to support them financially (See 2 Corinthians 8 & 9). "Let the elders that rule well be counted worthy of double honor (pay—author's parenthesis), especially those who labor in the word and doctrine. For the scripture says, "You shall not muzzle the ox that treads out the corn. And, the laborer is worthy of his hire." (1 Timothy. 5: 17-18). You don't pay a person to exercise his spiritual gift...he'll do that because he loves to...you pay him to set him free to minister. We also support them by assisting them in the work...Consider Luke, who himself apparently couldn't preach, but who could use his gift as a doctor to keep Paul healthy enough to do the preaching. He also used his gifts as a record keeper and writer (Luke and Acts). Words of encouragement are not wasted either.

4. The fourth invitation to the Christian is to make a **personal commitment** to: (a) pray for the lost, (b) witness to the lost, (c) enlist new church members, (d) accept a position of responsibility in the church, (e) begin to give finances, (f) etc. Their decision may be indicated by coming forward, standing, raised hand, signing a card, etc. It is perfectly scriptural to ask people to sign pledges (See Leviticus 27: 2; Numbers 30: 2; Psalms 22: 25; 66: 13; 116: 18; 65: 1: "Vow and pay unto the Lord your God: let all that be round about him bring presents unto him that ought to be feared." (g) Ask persons to commit their home to Christ...to begin a time of family

worship, etc.

The average church member doesn't value church membership because we have made it too easy to get in and too hard to get out. The churches that expect and demand excellence (the 2nd mile) from their membership are the ones that are growing numerically and spiritually.

An Evangelistic Invitation Defined

It is the appeal of one person to another to follow a definite course of action. This course of action may be one of the ten previously listed. It is the climactic moment when all that has gone before hangs in the balance. Many times, preachers deliver an excellent sermon, or witnesses give a powerful and effective testimony to God's saving power, and then destroy its effectiveness by not giving a clearly detailed invitation to respond to those who have listened. The difference between teaching and preaching is that preaching concludes with a "so what"—so what are you going to do about what you have heard? Hyman Appleman, an evangelist friend of mine, said, "The invitation is the stroke of the hammer driving the nail of the gospel into the heart of the hearer. An invitation brings to a focus, to a pointed summary, all that may have been said in the sermon." Appleman also said, "If properly given…it gives the Holy Spirit the greatest opportunity to probe the hearts, to search the souls, to expose them, their shortcomings, their foolish excuses to themselves."

F. D. Whitsell wrote: "Evangelistic preaching naturally culminates in an invitation. Without the invitation the evangelistic message is incomplete, and the effects of the message is an appeal to make a public response to the claims of Christ." Jesse M. Bader wrote: "Impression without expression is harmful." The invitation requires a great deal of energy and spiritual perception. I always feel that I am exhausted when I preach. I like the way Appleman described it. He said, "…in preaching of the word, you exhaust every resource of your brain, of your heart, of your soul, of your body." But even more exhausting than preaching is the invitation. Appleman described the invitation as "going the second mile to prostrate yourself, as it were before sinners, before backsliding Christians making a bridge out of your life for them to walk over out of hell into heaven..." Or, as Whitsell said, "More spiritual energy and compassion are needed in the invitation than in any other part of the evangelistic service."

Why Give a Public Invitation?

Our answer to this question is predicated upon our belief about the condition of mankind without Christ as personal Lord and Savior. That is a basic assumption that a person without Christ is now...not going to be...condemned to eternal hell (John 3: 18: "already condemned by a refusal—a refusal to believe in the name of the only begotten Son of God"). He is without the joy of forgiveness of sins, without the hope of eternal life, without the blessedness of having Christ in this life, and "without hope and without God in the world."

Whitsell wrote: "Unsaved people rarely look for a way to accept God's call, but rather a way to escape it. Men are running away from God rather than to Him. We must shut up the ways of escape and hedge these sinners to the straight and narrow way which leads to eternal life." (Consider Adam and Eve running away from God an as example).

An old man who had been to hear a preacher, told what it was like when the preacher gave no invitation. He described it as being "brought...right up face to face with the Judgment seat, and there he left us." The old man said, "There was no soft words to ease us down, such as, 'but I trust this is not true of you, brothers. 'Whitsell lists four reasons for giving a public invitation:

1. An invitation helps Christians to confess and forsake some known sin or failure that hurts them or hinders revival.

It gives immediate urgency to the plea that sinners turn to Christ today, right now.

2. It makes it easier for those who do trust Christ to confess Him openly.

3. It makes possible Scriptural instruction and counsel to those who decide for Christ.

4. I would like to add to that only one thing: In giving the invitation we catch the spirit of Christ and obey His command.

The Qualities of an Invitation

By qualities I mean how the invitation is to be given. Please take note that everything else I say about the invitation may be applied to either private or public invitations.

Sincerity is the first word I use in describing how to give an invitation. The word "sincere" has its base in the Latin language. It literally means "without wax." In the market place of that day pottery was sold. The wise buyer would hold up the piece of pottery to the sunlight, or place a light within the pottery, to see if there were flaws that had been filled with wax. The merchants would put up a sign over their merchandise saying "sincere" (sin=without + cere=wax). It carries the idea of "without cares." That is, when you are sincere you have no holes (no decay)...all wrong motives and desires are absent...you are acting from pure and unselfish motives. The invitation is not to be given for the purpose of padding statistics, getting another "notch in your spiritual gun," bringing praise to oneself or your church, etc. It should be given so that people's lives may be changed, that they may be saved from hell, that they may have eternal life, that this can be a better world, and, above all, that Christ may be glorified. Jarrette E. Aycock wrote: "...be careful to never leave a question or a doubt in anyone's mind as to your sincerity. You are dealing with immortal souls and on this dealing may hinge eternal life for someone."

CLARITY is the second word I use. Don't assume that people know what to do or how to do it. Spell it out clearly. Make your proposals distinct and separate in order for people to know why they are making a decision. If you study the great evangelists, you'll hear them say exactly what they want people to do. For example, Billy Graham would say something like this: "I'm going to ask you to get up from your seat and come down here and stand in front of me as an indication of your desire to turn your life to God. I'm going to ask you to do that right now. It will take you 3 minutes to come from the top rows, but we will wait. Your family or friends will wait for you. Come right now." That is clear.

FERVENTLY is the next word. As someone said, "Give the message of invitation to the people with a heart burning with the passion for the souls of all." If the matter isn't important enough for your heart to yearn for them, it is doubtful their heart will yearn for the life that Christ gives. The two men who walked with Christ on the road to Emmaus said, "Did not our hearts burn within us, while he talked with us by the way, and while he opened the scriptures?" (Lk. 24: 32). Is it not safe to say that, if we are filled with God's Spirit, we too, shall cause men's hearts to burn within them as we "open up the scriptures" ...that, as we fervently urge people to respond to Christ, they will desire to respond in a positive manner? Jesus promised us that we would do greater works than He did (John 14: 12). We should never let apparent failure on one occasion cause us to stop giving a fervent invitation on another occasion.

CONFIDENTLY is the fourth word I use. Expect people to respond to the invitation given in Christ's name. God will honor His word (2 Peter 3: 9; Isaiah. 55: 10-11). The story is told of a young preacher who asked C. H. Spurgeon, "Why do people not come forward when I give an invitation?" Mr. Spurgeon replied, "Do you expect someone to come forward every time you give an invitation?" "No, not every time," said the young preacher. "Well, no wonder they don't come," said Spurgeon.

HONESTLY is the fifth word to describe a powerful invitation. By honestly, I mean precisely. Tell people exactly what you want them to do...no more, no less. If you want them to raise their hand for prayer, tell them so, but if you want them to come forward and meet you, tell them that also. You may say something like, "After you have raised your hand for prayer, and we've prayed for you, then we'll give you an opportunity to come forward and openly declare what you've secretly decided." Also, once you make a promise during the invitation, be honest and keep it. If you say, "We'll sing one more stanza of a hymn, and if no one comes, we'll close." Close if no one comes. If someone comes, then you may feel free to say, "Since someone came, we'll sing another stanza." Or, if you are counseling or praying with someone who comes, the people will wait patiently...you need not say anything.

COURTEOUSLY is the sixth word of which I remind myself for the invitation. Don't embarrass people. I have seen on rare occasions men who are discourteous, embarrassing many in the audience. They may say something like, "I want everyone who is a Christian to turn around and face the back of the auditorium." Then when the Christians had turned around, and others honestly admitted they weren't Christians by not turning, the evangelist would then say, "Now, all of you who are Christians are looking a lost man in the eyes." It may be that God sometimes uses shocking realities to turn people to Himself, but I doubt that man has the right to do that. A certain man who became a Christian in his senior years, once told me, "I probably would have come to Christ sooner if an evangelist hadn't once told me to go ahead and go to hell." Then he explained how the evangelist got him out of bed to witness to him. When he refused to make a positive decision, the evangelist had tried to shock him by saying, "If that's the way you feel, then go ahead and go to hell." Someone once said, "The Holy Spirit is a gentleman. He knocks at the door, but He doesn't knock it down." Should we go beyond the methods of the Holy Spirit?

EARNESTLY is word number seven. I will use "urgently" as a synonym for this word. Don't ever make such an important thing just a matter of fact...a convenient way to close the service. Two things are evident here: one, the person to whom you are speaking may never have another opportunity to make a positive decision, and, two, you may never have another opportunity to invite him to make such a positive decision for Christ. (You do realize, don't you, that people make some kind of decision every time the Holy Spirit confronts them? I remember the government official from Vietnam that I shared the gospel with saying, "Wayne, I understand, but I work for a Communist government, and I have no choice." When he said that he had just made a choice—the wrong one.)

PLEADINGLY is word number eight. Don't be ashamed to make a fool of yourself for the sake of Christ. Plead as "a dying man with dying men."

PRAYERFULLY is the ninth word. Jarrette Aycock wrote: "Depend upon God for the seed, the sunshine and the rain, and the glorious harvest. Never depend upon man, or upon man's message for these." I confess that I still don't know the full power of the prayer of a righteous man, but I do know that the time of invitation is a battle against Satan…a battle that must be won in prayer before one even preaches, much as less, to give an invitation.

USE MUCH SCRIPTURE is a phrase that sums up the tenth idea in giving a powerful invitation. Quote Scripture promises made to the lost person. Absolutely nothing convicts the lost person's heart like the Word of God. F. D. Whitsell wrote: "Quotations from the Word of God have a peculiar power to arrest the attention and to drive home divine truths. A few well-chosen scriptural quotations make an invitation more forceful and gripping." Remember in Acts 2 on the Day of Pentecost that Peter used many other words in persuading the crowd, and I'm sure some were words of scripture. Once I was sharing the gospel with a lady in her home. When I had explained the gospel, I asked her, "Is there any reason you cannot give your heart to the Lord Jesus right now?" She replied, "Yes, there are too many hypocrites in the church." I knew many human arguments related to that excuse. However, God's Spirit led me to use none of man's arguments. Therefore, I said, "May I quote several verses of scripture?" She agreed to listen. I gave her a paraphrase of Matthew 7: 1-5… "Judge not, that you be not judged.

For with what judgment you judge, you shall be judged: and with what measure you mete, it shall be measured to you again. And why do you behold the toothpick in your brother's eye when you have a two-by-four in your own eye? You hypocrite, first get the two-by-four out of your own eye; then you'll be able to see to get the toothpick out of your brother's eye." After quoting that passage, I asked, "Now, who does God call the hypocrite?" She replied, "Me." I then asked her again if she was ready to ask the Lord to save her. She broke out into a beautiful prayer and acknowledged Jesus as Lord of her life.

INNOVATIVELY is word number eleven. Be alert to any honorable method by which you can get people to make a positive decision for Christ. The Holy Spirit taught me a lesson in this when I was preaching in South Africa. The custom of the churches there at the time of the invitation was to sing one hymn and sing it only one time through. Therefore, the time of invitation was many times too brief. On this occasion, I knew there were many who wanted to make a positive decision for Christ, but for one reason or another, had not done so. Therefore, I said, "I am sure that many of you wanted to respond positively to Christ as your Lord tonight. So, after our closing prayer, the pastor will stand at the door to greet those of you who had no decision to make. However, for those of you who wanted to make a decision, but haven't yet, I am going to ask you to remain in your seat, and we'll have a counselor to come to you and answer your questions and to pray with you." The first time I tried this it was very exciting. There had been four people who came forward during the singing of the hymn. Yet, we counseled forty-four additional people after the service. That meant that forty-four additional people made positive decisions for Christ that night that wouldn't have done so had not the Holy Spirit led me to be innovative. That one service became a pattern for all of the remaining services I led in South Africa.

Also, I have learned at business club meetings where I preach to lead them to pray to receive Christ, there is no opportunity for a "come forward" invitation. I simply ask them, if they received Christ, to leave their business card on the table. I have been able to mail follow-up material to literally hundreds of businessmen that otherwise would have made no decision. If you will sincerely ask the Holy Spirit to lead you, He will make you very innovative. I did a similar thing in a theatre where there was no room to have a come forward invitation only to see hundreds remain in their seats until we could pray with them to receive Christ as Lord and Savior.

The Length of the Invitation

There is no issue that is more trying to the preacher's spirit (whether in a corporate worship service or in a private interview) than this one of how long to continue to persuade persons to make a positive decision for Christ. It is an issue that each person must decide between him and God's Holy Spirit. However, there a few scriptural guidelines that are helpful. I have three things for your consideration.

> **Length of Invitation**
>
> Careful planning
>
> Scriptural pattern:
>
> Many other words of testimony and exhortation

One, the length of the invitation requires **careful planning**. While one cannot plan a certain number of minutes or stanzas of a song, planning is still helpful. The leadership of the Holy Spirit must be sensed (felt or experienced) at the time of the invitation. It should be He that dictates the amount of time allotted. So, what do I mean by planning then? I mean, plan the time of your presentation (sermon or private interview) so that you have sufficient time for the invitation when your sermon is over. It is better to decrease the time of presentation than to lose souls for the Master, because you didn't have enough time left for the invitation. Plan how you are going to transition from the message to the invitation. Plan how you are going to give it—raised hands, come forward, sign a card, or all of the above. Plan what motivation you will use—fear of loss, promise of gain, etc. Plan what you are going to say and how you are going to say it. The Holy Spirit is master of your planning the same way He is controller of your spontaneity. If the Holy Spirit wants you to do something different than you planned, He knows your address and phone number. He has promised to guide you in all truth when you present the truth.

Two, when considering the length of the invitation, as in all matters, consider the scriptural pattern as used by Simon Peter on the Day of Pentecost. Don't apologize for taking time to persuade people to respond positively to Christ. Don't let cold, unconcerned criticism of non-evangelists, cause you to cut short the time of invitation. Follow the example of Simon Peter that he set on that blessed day when 3,000 people came to Christ..." And with many other words did he testify and exhort, saying, save yourselves from this untoward generation" (Acts 2: 40). Notice that he used "many other words." While his sermon was relatively short, his invitation was relatively long. After his brief sermon, he now turns to invite people to come to Christ—the invitation was being given, and he waited for people to decide for or against Christ. He used many other words to persuade them. John Bisagno once said, "Most of the decisions for Christ are made after the fifth stanza of a hymn." What kind of words did Peter use? Words of testimony and exhortation. He used words of testimony. Don't apologize for personal references--that's what you know the most about. If anyone says to you, "That's bragging," agree with them, and say to them, "Yes, it is bragging, but it is bragging on Jesus, not about me." He also used words of exhortation (encouragement). Many times, a person needs a little more encouragement to step across the line. Exhortation also includes words of wisdom. That means to give advice; to give a word to the wise; to prompt or persuade; to counsel or instruct; to prescribe or to recommend; to teach and to guide. Certainly, there is room within the meaning of exhortation to take time (whatever time is necessary) to deal with people about their relationship to Christ—about their eternal destiny. There are many who have become angry with me for giving a "long invitation," but there are many who will meet me in heaven and thank me for extending the time of invitation a little longer. Often during the invitation, I make that as a disarming strategy.

Three, the length of the invitation should be governed by the command of our Lord. "And the Lord said, "Go out into the highways and hedges, and compel them to come in, that my house may be filled." (Lk. 14: 23). I find five distinct things is this command: (1) the authority for the invitation. In this story the master represents God. He is the authority for us giving an invitation. What greater right do we need?

(2) The testator of the invitation is any believer who is a servant of Christ. If you call yourself a servant of Christ, then you are commanded to invite people to Christ--give an invitation. (3) The location of the invitation is "the highways and the hedges" (where the lost people are). There is compelling evidence that we're not getting lost people into the churches to hear the gospel. Only about 3 percent of those in church are unchurched. (4) There is the manner of the invitation... "compel them to come in." The word "compel" carries the idea of coercion, constraint, enforcement, draft, pin down, bind, etc. If people accuse you of pressuring them into a decision, say, "I plead guilty...I am pressuring you. However, don't get angry with me...I'm only doing as I am told by the Lord Jesus Christ. Plus, I am doing it for your eternal good." However, remember the command is to be carried out in love... "The love of Christ constrains us" (2 Cor. 5: 14). Isn't it interesting that we are constrained to constrain? (5) There is the purpose of the invitation, namely, to assure that heaven is full ("That my house may be full"). Our Lord wants his house filled. Not just his earthly house, the church building, but primarily his heavenly house that He is preparing (See John 14). God is interested in numbers—He put a whole book in the Bible named Numbers. Don't fall prey to the devil's lie: "we're more interested in quality, not quantity." God is interested in both. Getting quantity builds the quality...getting the quality is no guarantee of quantity. Many groups have become

ingrown and stagnant because they have emphasized their growth to the neglect of the growth of God's church. These people remind me of the couples who are "going to wait until they can afford to have children." You don't get to the place of affordability. It remains a fact that new converts will grow us up faster than designed courses of study. I believe in discipleship. In fact, I have a growth book (Now That You Are a Christian), and a commentary on that growth book (Caring for the Needs of the Newborn Believer), which can be ordered through Amazon.com. However, discipleship is not just learning what Jesus said. It is also doing what He said. He reached out to the multitudes. If we are to be like Him, we must also reach out and invite people to come to Him.

The Methods of the Invitation

How do you get people to decide for Christ? In a real sense, we don't get them to decide for Christ. Only the Holy Spirit can do that. On the other hand, the Holy Spirit uses human agents to persuade people to decide for Christ. So, what motives do we give people when we ask them to turn to God from sin? There are four basic appeals: basic drives, motives, principles, epitome. I'll explain these.

We motivate people by appealing to their basic **drives**. What are these basic drives?

> **FIVE PRINCIPLES FROM JESUS ABOUT THE INVITATION**
>
> The Authority for invitations is Jesus
>
> Any person can invite people to Jesus
>
> Location is where lost people are
>
> Manner is to compel
>
> Purpose is to fill heaven

There is the desire for **self-preservation**. Satan had pretty well read people in general when he accused Job to God, saying, "Skin for skin, yea, all that a man has will he give for his life" (Job 2: 4). We know there are times when most people will give up themselves for the protection of another (i.e. a mother for her child, a man for his wife, a person for his country, etc.). However, there is in all of us a desire to protect self. This desire may be expressed in a wrong way, but in itself, it is good and necessary. Think what the suicide rate would be if God didn't give to mankind a natural fear of death. As one man facetiously said, "I'm not afraid of dying; I just don't want to be on the next load." So, we appeal to people by promising them eternal life through Jesus Christ.

The next basic appeal through which we approach people is for **personal happiness.** All people want to find bliss, felicity, enjoyment and pleasure in life. Through Jesus Christ we can offer them bliss without end, felicity without alloy, enjoyment without remorse, and pleasure without regret. Outside of Christ there is no lasting happiness.

Another drive to which we may appeal is **recognition**. Each person has an innate need for praise and prestige. We all need some approval from others. The alert evangelist will show people that as they relate their life to Christ, they become known to the greatest Being in the universe, Almighty God. Jesus said, "My sheep hear my voice, and I know them, and they follow me" (John 10: 27-29). What a wonderful recognition comes to God's children who serve Him faithfully. Jesus pointed to a day of commendation and approval when He told us that on that day God would say to us, "Well done, good and faithful servant: you have been faithful over a few things, I will make you ruler over many things: enter into the joy of your Lord" (Matt. 25: 21).

The fourth basic drive is **security.** There is none who don't desire safety, protection, preservation…a guardian angel. We can announce to people that God provides all of these: safety… "I will both lay me down in peace and sleep; for you, Lord, only make me dwell in safety" (Psalm 4: 8); preservation… "And the Lord shall deliver me from every evil work, and will preserve me unto His heavenly kingdom: to whom be glory forever and ever: (2 Timothy 4: 18); protection… "I give them eternal life; and they shall never perish, neither shall any man pluck them out of my hand" (John 10: 28); and, a guardian angel... "But to which of the angels said he at any time, Sit on my right hand, until I make your enemies your footstool? Are they not all ministering spirits, sent forth to minister for them who shall be heirs of salvation? (Hebrews 1: 13-14).

A fifth appeal is **freedom**...free in three ways...free from condemnation, free to the power of God, and free to experience God's presence. Sin has a condemning effect in our life. Every individual experiences this condemnation. But because of Jesus Christ we can be free from that condemnation... "There is therefore now no condemnation to them which are in Christ Jesus, who walk not after the flesh, but after the Spirit. For the law of the Spirit of life in Christ Jesus has made me free from the law of sin and death" (Romans 8: 1-2). Sin has a dominating effect in our life, also. But in Christ Jesus we are free from "the power of sin..." "And you shall know the truth, and the truth shall make you free...If the Son therefore makes you free, you shall be free indeed" (John 8: 32, 36). Again, in Christ Jesus we will one day be set free from the presence of sin... "Now unto him that is able to keep you from falling (free from sin's power: author's parenthesis), and to present you faultless before the presence of His glory with exceeding joy, (free from sin's presence: author's parenthesis) (Jude 24)...Nevertheless we, according to His promise, look for new heavens and a new earth, wherein dwells righteousness" (2 Peter 3: 13).

A sixth basic appeal is the desire for **adventure**. If Christ can offer anything it is a life of adventure. He is indeed the Lord of surprises. What intriguing adventure may be seen in a study of any of God's great heroes! This is true in the Bible and in post-biblical history. Please read Jesus' description of a life of adventure as recorded in Matthew, chapters five through seven.

A seventh basic appeal is desire for **satisfaction**. Life in Christ is somewhat of a paradox...it is extremely satisfying, yet one always longs for more. It is being satiated without being nauseated. It leaves no hunger or thirst... "Jesus said unto them, I am the bread of life; he that comes to me shall never hunger; and he that believes in Me shall never thirst" (John 6: 35). Jesus gives satisfaction that leaves no hangovers.

An eighth appeal is **to be loved**. Millions today feel like the Psalmist when he said, "I looked on my right hand, and behold, but there was no man that would know me: refuge failed me: no man cared for my soul" (Psalm 142: 4). To these millions we can declare that in Christ and in His church, they will find love… "The Lord has appeared of old unto me, saying, I have loved you with an everlasting love; therefore, with loving-kindness have I drawn you" (Jeremiah 31: 3). "By this shall all men know that you are my disciples, if you have love for one another" (John 13: 35).

Next, there are many motives mankind has; therefore, we can use the **motive** appeal. As we make appeals to persons to accept Christ as Lord and Savior, there are some basic assumptions.

Basic Assumptions About the Invitation

First, ,we must assume that it is an agreement with the basic concepts of life to think that being a Christian is not out of the ordinary. As George Sweazey wrote: "The basic assumption of evangelism is always this: IT IS NORMAL TO BE A CHRISTIAN; IT IS ABNORMAL TO BE AWAY FROM CHRIST." We need to avow daily, even hourly, that the abnormal or unnatural person is the person who is living apart from God. A person who doesn't know Christ as Lord is not what God made him to be. He has not fulfilled his purpose for existence.

Second, there are needed different approaches for different people. As the modern-day statement goes: "different strokes for different folks." As Sweazey put it, "Access to a human soul is like access to a mountain peak. Some, including very lofty ones, offer many easy approaches. Others are craggy and difficult. Like Alpinists who circle a peak to find the least forbidding path, so the evangelist must often go all around a person, looking for the point of access."

Third, there are no certain approaches. We can't assume that everyone recognizes the longings of his soul to be a thirst for God. Nor can we assume that all people are laden with the guilt of their sins. We can't take for granted that every person who is lost appreciates Christian fellowship or is tired of secular living. Some even enjoy it. Because of this it is very difficult for a church to specialize in one way of approaching people with the gospel. It may be fine for doctors to become specialists, but the church must remain a general practitioner. We must "become all thing to all men that we may thereby reach some" (1 Corinthians 9: 20-22). This is true for individual witnesses also.

Fourth, we must assume that God has provided some way to approach every person. If one way fails, we must try another. As Sweazey said, "Faith often makes its entry through a very narrow beachhead." The beachhead can be enlarged once we have established it. Perhaps, the fisherman left their nets out of fascination with Jesus, but, if they did, they later called Him their Lord. If someone only sees Him as an example today, then, tomorrow he may see Jesus Christ as Lord and Savior. Those who come to Christ because of a crisis in their life may soon come because of a genuine love for Him...One who sees God as a benevolent maker through nature may be led to see Him as a beneficial master through nurture.

Fifth, we are to assume that God wants each of us to make some kind of appeal to those we know. It is ours to knock on the heart-door of each person. It is the Holy Spirit's to enforce the knocking that it may be heard. It is theirs to open or close the door. But it is God's to cause them to open the door. Only He can open the heart of an unbeliever. We are to make sure that the lack of a beachhead does not lie in our failure to launch our artillery units.

What then are the motive appeals we can make? In the following paragraphs I will give a composite list of these appeals. I suggest you weave one or more of these motives into each of your messages.

Motive Appeals

1. **Deliverance from the sense of sin**…relief of guilt is one of these appeals. Christians who are close to God are deeply aware of their sins and are grateful for the forgiveness that is found in Christ. However, the lost person may or may not have a sense of his sins. Sweazey said, "Evangelism cannot always go with the good news of salvation to those who don't know they are lost; it must go with the bad news to those who think they are doing well." As my seminary professor would often say, "Fellows, you have to get them lost before you can get them saved." Many are discouraged by their failures, others are dogged by their guilt, and still others cringe from their weakness. To these we may say that a right relationship to God through Jesus Christ relieves all of these symptoms. On the other hand, to those who believe they are doing as well as can be expected under the circumstances, we need to go with the message that "all have sinned and come short of the glory of God" (Romans 3: 23). And when they are convinced of that we can assure them of God's love and His provision for the sinner to be forgiven and saved eternally.

2. **Hope in the midst of chaos** is another motive appeal. To a world that fears inflation, fuel and food shortages, the threat of war or terrorism, dishonest men in government, pollution, and a thousand other ills we can offer hope. We can announce that God's plan of economy is sure; that God never forsakes the righteous… "I have been young, and now am old; yet have I not seen the righteous forsaken, nor his seed begging bread" (Psalm 37: 25); that God and His people will be the ultimate victors in the final war; that God can make dishonest people honest, and that God will ultimately create a new world where pollution is not known---wherein dwells righteousness.

3. A third motive appeal is the **dread of impersonal forces**. Although many may not in this "enlightened age" look upon demons and powers of darkness as our forefathers did (I am not among those; I know the reality of such impersonal forces, having done spiritual warfare with them on many occasions), modern people still fear the unseen and unknown. And, well they might, according to Ephesians 6: 10-18. Literally hundreds of thousands of people rush through this life with anxious backward glances fearing dreaded omens of disaster. These people will listen to anything which offers them deliverance from this state of foreboding. The message of evangelism which Christ has committed to us can give these people the assurance that God is still in control of this universe...that He has not abdicated His throne to anyone or anything, nor is He about to abdicate. We can promise them that the destiny of the world is still in God's hands...that He is the God of the future as He has been the God of the past... "Jesus Christ the same yesterday, and today, and forever" (Hebrews 13: 8). We can offer them securities upon which people can rely... "In the world you shall have tribulation but be of good cheer; I have overcome the world" (John 16: 31). We can assure them that nothing can separate us from the love of God which is in Christ Jesus (Romans 8: 38-39).

4. There is the motive appeal of **relief from anxiety**. Millions are beset by insecurity. They fear the loss of their jobs, insufficient money to live on a standard level, not being loved, losing a family member, or losing their health. To these people the message of Christ can give assurances that can be found in no other place.

5. Again, there is the motive appeal of **victory over lost assurances**. In a world of chaos and confusion people need certainty and confidence. They need more than a "hope so" or "think so" religion...they need a "know so" faith in Jesus Christ. To these people we can say with certainty and confidence that in Christ there is assurance. (Incidentally, I have a commentary, not yet in print, on the Epistle of First John, giving about 20 reasons for assurance— pray with me about printing it).

6. A sixth motive appeal is **freedom from boredom.** So many people get up from their sleep each day having nothing for which to look forward. They aren't sure that their life contributes anything worthwhile. Even their recreation and pleasures yield no fun. Much of the obesity and anxiety that plague Americans is the result of boredom. Suicide is another scourge that finds much of its roots in boredom. The New Testament word for sin means "a missed aim." That is the state from which Jesus Christ, with His exciting and challenging purposes, delivers us.

6. **Forgiveness of sins** is the seventh motive appeal. That means to take the offense that stands between us and someone else, including God, and put it behind us so that it doesn't affect our relationship to each other. With so much between people and God this is one of the major appeals. Psychiatrists have agreed that "eighty percent of the people in hospitals for care of sickness could walk away healthy if they had their sins forgiven." To these and others, we can announce: "The blood of Jesus His Son cleanses us from all sin" (1 John 1: 7b). We can assure them that God has buried their sins in the deepest sea.

7. An eighth motive appeal is that **Christ needs us; we need Christ.** God can get along without people (Acts 17: 24-25).However, He has chosen to augment His working with people by the works of others. The poet said, "God has no hands but our hands to do His work today; He has no feet but our feet to lead men in His way; He has no tongue but our tongues to tell men how He died; He has no people but this people to lead them to His side." In that sense, He needs us. As to our need of Him, I cannot write enough lines to describe that. Suffice it to say, we were made to belong to Him; in Him we live and move and breathe and have our being; were He to withdraw His hand from our lives we would cease to exist. The song writer had it right when he wrote "I Need Thee Every Hour."

8. **Self-perplexity** is a ninth motive appeal. People are puzzled and embarrassed by themselves. Each time we look within we are confronted by the troubling riddle of our existence. We can reach

many people by answering where people came from, why they are here, and where they are going (See my book *How to Know and Grow in Christ* for the answers to these questions). The New Testament answers these questions. As to questions that are unanswerable, we can point ourselves and them to a confidence in God's providential care. And we can be like the Psalmist who wrote: "Lord, my heart is not proud; my eyes are not haughty. I do not get involved with things too great or too difficult for me. Instead, I have calmed and quieted myself like a little weaned child with its mother; I am like a little child" (Psalm 131: 1-2).

9. **Fulfillment of God's purpose (God's will)** is a tenth motive appeal. People are wondering: "What does God want from me?" Evangelism answers this question from God's Word. God wants people to be just, to love kindness and to walk humbly with Him" (Micah 6: 8).

10. **A new life (a new person)** is an eleventh motive appeal. Many are disgusted with what they are and what they have been. Their past holds a dark gloom; their present is clouded; and their future is dim. In this stormy condition our message declares, "If any man is in Christ, he is a new creature; old thing are passed away; behold, all things are become new" (2 Corinthians 5: 17). When a person comes to Christ, he doesn't get a new lease on life...he gets a new life. He doesn't turn over a new leaf...he gets a whole new book.

11. **The fear of death** is a twelfth motive appeal. Job's question, "if a man die, shall he live again?" is still much on the minds of all people. With all of the talk about life after death people want some concrete answers. With the message of resurrection from the dead so plain in the New Testament, we have an undeniable avowal that man shall live again indeed. We can say with Job, "I wish that my words were written down, that they were recorded on a scroll or were inscribed in a stone forever by an iron stylus and lead! But I know my living Redeemer, (alternate translation: I know that my Redeemer lives), and He will stand on the dust at last. Even after my skin has been destroyed, yet I will see God in my flesh. I will see

Him myself; with my eyes will I look at Him, and not as a stranger. My heart longs within me" (Job 19: 23-27).

12. **Loneliness** is the thirteenth motive appeal. The cry of the Psalmist, "I looked on my right hand, and beheld, but there was no man that would know me: refuge failed me; no man cared for my soul" (Psalm 142: 4), is the cry of many today. They are lonely because no one has found them. This is why so many meets over the internet. They are not able to make any meaningful contacts with other human beings. In Christ we can offer a double answer to loneliness. First, we can give a real fellowship in which people can know and love each other. Second, we can bring together the lonely one and the Father who has been searching for him. Added to that, we can bring him into the church where he will find friends, purpose and closeness.

I remember when I was a child. My sister took me to the Sugar Bowl in New Orleans for a football game. After the game, she told me to stand in one place and wait for her. She was gone for what seemed to me to be a long time. There were thousands of people walking through the tunnels of the stadium, but I didn't know any of them. It was there that I first experienced the daunting fear of loneliness. I was in a crowd of thousands, but I felt all alone. Many people feel this intense loneliness and will welcome a caring person into their life. This speaks of the effectiveness of door-to-door visitation, as well as the appeal to lonely people who hear you witness or preach. Assure these folks that with Jesus Christ they are never alone.

13. **The promises of God** is still another motive appeal. Someone has pointed out that there are enough promises in the Bible, God's Word, that a person can claim a new one every day and not use them all up in a number of years.

14. **The sense of something lacking** is the fifteenth motive appeal. People want something that is beyond this world. There is always a growing consciousness that something is not complete in this life. While we cannot compete with the world in entertainment, we can

bring a message from beyond this world. As Sweazey said, "If it (the church) can really connect people with something (Someone) which is greater than themselves, they will come to it (the church)."

15. **Hunger for truth** is one more motive appeal. Pilate said, "What is truth?" (John 18: 38). In a world of relative values and situation ethics many are seeking something that is solid and plain. As Lord Halifax said, "Men will not be brought to embrace Christian religion because it is recommended expedient, or necessary, or full of moral values. But they will go on their knees if they can come to feel that it is true." Or, as Sweazey wrote: "Unless there is such a God as Christianity describes, there are no good reasons for going to church; if there is such a God, there are no good reason for staying away."

16. **Appeal for oneness of the family** is still another motive appeal. We need to be careful at this point. However, it is valid to tell a person that his family can be complete in eternity through faith in Jesus Christ. All who are reborn through faith in Christ will be one family in eternity, but most people want their earthly family to be together forever. I know I want to see my father and mother and brothers, etc., but I also want to see Abraham, Noah, David, John, Peter, etc., but most of all, I want to see Jesus.

17. **The idea of doing or being better** is another motive appeal in evangelism. Every person has said to himself or herself at one time or another: "I don't like me very well." People want to be a better parent or employee or employer or son or daughter. They want to do a better job of all they try. Our message declares to them that God and we love them "warts and all" (Churchill when his portrait was being done), and that we'll help them become what God and they want to become.

18. **The assurance of God's existence and presence (the missing significance of God)** is a powerful motive appeal. There are not a great many real atheists among us, but there are millions of practical atheists. The real atheist says with his lips that there is

no God. The practical atheist (Psalm 14: 1) says in his heart there is a God but lives his life as if there was not a God. Also, many who really believe in God do not see Him at work in their daily lives. Once, we lead a person to Christ, and he is born again, he knows his God to be the Living God, and finds comfort therein. Jesus told us that if any person will do what God wants, that person will know for sure of the doctrine (the teachings of the Bible), whether it is from God or whether it was from the earthly man Jesus alone (John 17: 7). We can assure them that they will understand the Bible once they know the Author. Many are drawn by a motive appeal **to sacrifice something for God**. Most young people, including young adults, are looking for a hands-on form of Christianity (going on a short-term mission—digging water wells, health clinics, relief excursions, etc.). They desire to give themselves to a cause bigger than self. These wish to be involved in the heroic. The advancement of Christ's kingdom offers that cause…that heroism.

19. Many others are attracted to Christ because they have **a mistrust of life**. Millions of people feel that the universe is hostile and that life is cruel…that God, if there is such a Being, is vindictive, or, at least, indifferent to human needs. They see natural disasters and man-made genocide as evidence of their ideas of God's "cruelty to the human race." We can proclaim to these folks that God is on their side…that He is working on their behalf, and has wonderful things in store for them ("For I know the plans I have for you—this is the Lord's declaration—plans for your welfare, not for disaster, to give you a future and a hope": Jeremiah 29: 11). We can say to them: "God is love" (1 John 4: 8). **Strength for temptation** is another motive appeal to use in reaching people for God. Some have lost so many battles with a particular temptation that they despair of ever winning over their weaknesses. To these we can declare that they have lost some battles, but Jesus has won the war…and through Him they can also win. We can refer them to Matthew 4 where they can learn how Jesus quoted the Bible to overcome temptations. We can show them that God will not permit

their temptation to be too great for them but will provide an escape from said temptation ("No temptation has overtaken you except what is common to humanity. God is faithful, and He will not allow you to be tempted beyond what you are able, but with the temptation He will also provide a way of escape so that you are able to bear it" 1 Corinthians 10: 13). Verse 14 shows us that sometimes the way to handle the temptation is to get out of there ("Therefore, my dear friends, <u>flee</u> from idolatry…").

20. **Inner conflict** is another valid motive appeal. The evidence that people have needs here is seen in the fact that a book entitled *"Peace of Mind"* immediately became a best seller. The message of Christ says to those who are torn by conflict, "You shall find rest unto your souls: (See context in Matthew 11: 28-30). To those who are driven to distraction and discord, we may declare that Christ will give to them quietness and confidence and help…that they can have a peace that passes human understanding (See Philippians 4: 4-7, which declares that we should worry about nothing, pray about anything, and thank God for everything, and we will have peace that exceeds human understanding, even if the circumstances don't change).

21. **An appeal to use their influence rightly** is still another motive appeal. We may say to people what Mordecai said to Esther during her exceedingly difficult circumstances: "…who knows whether you are come to the kingdom for such a time as this?" (Esther 4: 14b). Jesus' command to let our light shine (Matthew 5: 16) was not so much a command for shining, but a command as to the manner of our light shining. Our light will shine (we all have influence)—it just depends on the form it takes (what our influence will be). In Christ we can have the right kind of influence.

22 The twenty-fifth motive appeal is the **resentment of material domination.** Many have come to the place of resenting the "keeping up with the Joneses." Others resent being put upon by high-speed living. To these we can declare that Christ is the constant in a rapidly changing world ("Jesus Christ, the same

yesterday, and today, and forever").

23. Many have an **eagerness for a better world.** This, too, is a good motive appeal. There is a desire for social change. The church of Jesus Christ has done more to blast tyranny, and to force open the doors to enlightenment, health and freedom for countless multitudes than any other earthly institution. Christ has done more for womanhood than anyone else in human history. We can say to people with total assurance that Christ through them and us can bring these needed changes into our world.

24. There is a **craving for brotherhood.** This, too, is a valid motive appeal. We can never have the brotherhood of man without the fatherhood of God. Many want to see change but feel too weak to accomplish anything. Therefore, they feel the need for joining with a group of people to accomplish a common goal. Christianity offers a brotherhood (sisterhood) like nothing else in the world. It is the message of Christ when accepted that brings about the brotherhood of mankind.

25. Then there is the **admiration of Jesus Christ** that is a motive appeal to many. This is our most powerful appeal. It is involved in all the other appeals. People, for the most part, will criticize Christians and the church, but will not criticize Christ. This gives us a common ground from which to work together to change our world for the better.

26. I love the next motive appeal. It is the **power of the cross (the power of the gospel unto salvation unto everyone who believes).** This greatest appeal that Christ has for mankind is not His example, nor His teachings, nor His heroism. His greatest appeal is His sacrificial death...the innocent for the guilty; the pure for the filthy; the sinless for the sinner...Men find power in His shed blood to break the shackles of sin, to put their homes back together, to be freed from guilt and shame, and to have purpose and meaning in life. As Jesus said, "And I, if I be lifted up from the earth, will draw all men unto me" (John 12: 32).

27. It would be great if you decide to take one of these motives into each of your presentations. Aim your presentation toward that appeal, and then, invite people to come to Christ with confidence, and without apology. Your church will experience change if you plan and do the Lord's invitation to His glory and for their benefit.

Here a few **questionable appeals**. I fear these four can easily be misused. There are not always wrong, but they are ones that can be used to manipulate people rather than to invite them. The first is **fear.** I believe this is a valid motive for man to repent. I also believe it is valid to use as an appeal. However, I feel that we should mention only those God-given fears used in the Bible, and not fears concocted by people. It is scriptural to talk about Divine justice, judgment and wrath, and the awesome fact of a fiery hell, but I think it is wrong to frighten people with fear of the hydrogen bomb, economic disorder, etc. As one minister put it, "I would rather frighten them into heaven than to soothe them into hell."

> OUR PURPOSE IN PREACHING
>
> IS NOT TO SHOW OFF OUR
>
> SKILLS, BUT TO PERSUADE
>
> PEOPLE TO BECOME
>
> DISCIPLES OF JESUS CHRIST

28. A second questionable motive appeal is **social pressure**. This can be improperly used. For example, consider the following statements: "We want every member of this class to join the church"; "you know how happy it would make your spouse (mother, father, etc.); "you're the only one who hasn't made a decision." Examples may be used to have some influence, but unless we keep it in a secondary position, we will be receiving people who consent to call themselves Christians solely on the basis of a desire to conform or to please others, instead of being based on true

repentance of sin and faith in the Lord Jesus Christ. The third questionable appeal is **worldly motives,** such as: "Our church is a good place to make good business contacts:" "We have the city champs in softball every year"; etc. Such motives do not glorify our Lord and Savior. The final questionable appeal that I will mention is **superstition**. God is more than a talisman or a good-luck charm. Some person testifies that his business began to grow when he made Christ his Lord, and many will think that God is a good business associate. There is an element of truth to this, but God is not interested in being an associate—He is Lord. This is certainly a secondary motive at best. In evangelism we may declare there is a principle of persuasion. It is "a good to be gained; an evil to be avoided." In persuading people to receive Christ we may point to the difference between many alternatives (for example: assurance or fear; fellowship or loneliness, etc.). Let's become all things to all people that we may by all means save some. However, let us never compromise the message of the gospel.

29. Perhaps, one more word is needed. Practice discipleship evangelism instead of shallow evangelism. Christianity is not "easy-believism". It is a commitment to the Lordship of Christ. In fact, we are not authorized to invite people to accept Jesus as Savior. We are authorized to invite them to make Jesus their Lord, and when they do make Him their Lord, He becomes their Savior ("If you will say with your mouth that Jesus is Lord, and believe in your heart that God raised Him from the dead, you shall be saved (have a Savior) (Romans 10: 9). This is not to preach "lordship salvation." It is to make sure that we understand that we cannot receive Jesus as Savior as an insurance policy against hell, and then when we are through with our rough living, we can then make Him our Lord, as well. It is to ensure that we make Him Lord of our life and trust Him to save us for all eternity. Whether people totally agree with all I have said about the invitation is not at all important. It is important that we all adopt some method of inviting people to Christ. We are to be intentional in practicing biblical evangelism. The churches of

today are static, at best, and dying, at worst, because we have shelved biblical evangelism. Wouldn't you rather have people criticize you for being aggressive in evangelism than to hear the Savior say, "You wicked and slothful servant…take away his talents and give them to the one who has ten, for I know the one who has the ten he has used will use the additional talents I give unto him?"

God bless you for the sake of souls hanging in the balance between heaven and hell. God bless you for the sake of our Lord Jesus Christ who died to deliver souls from hell. God bless you for the many you will take along with you when you approach the bema judgment seat of Christ.

May you hear his "WELL DONE, GOOD AND FAITHFUL SERVANT. YOU HAVE BEEN FAITHFUL IN A FEW THINGS: ENTER INTO THE JOY OF YOUR LORD!"

SUGGESTED READING

(Sources from which I have gathered these materials)

Evangelism in a Changing America by Jesse M. Bader

Personal Evangelism by F. Carlton Booth

An Interpretation of the English Bible by B. H. Carroll

Systematic Theology by Louis Sperry Chafer

Lectures on Revivals of Religion by Charles G. Finney

Effective Evangelism by Roland Q. Leavell

Dealing with the Devil by C. S. Lovett

Expositions of the Holy Scriptures by Alexander MacClaren

The Burden of the Lord by Ian MacPherson

Every Christian's Job by C. E. Matthews

The Way to God and How to Find It by D. L. Moody

Baptist Beliefs by E. Y. Mullins

Touch of the Spirit-Filled Approach to Witnessing by Ralph W. Neighbour

Lectures to My Students by C. H. Spurgeon

Basic Christianity by John R. W. Stott

The Effective Invitation by R. Alan Street

Preaching the Good News by George Sweazey

Other Sources: Classroom notes by Vernon L. Stanfield, Gordon Johnson, and Charles McKay.

Made in the USA
Middletown, DE
14 April 2019